DANNY LONDON

A TRUE STORY

john j. morabito

TATE PUBLISHING
AND ENTERPRISES, LLC

Danny London
Copyright © 2016 by John J. Morabito. All rights reserved.

No part of this publication may be reproduced, stored in a retrieval system or transmitted in any way by any means, electronic, mechanical, photocopy, recording or otherwise without the prior permission of the author except as provided by USA copyright law.

This book is designed to provide accurate and authoritative information with regard to the subject matter covered. This information is given with the understanding that neither the author nor Tate Publishing, LLC is engaged in rendering legal, professional advice. Since the details of your situation are fact dependent, you should additionally seek the services of a competent professional.

The opinions expressed by the author are not necessarily those of Tate Publishing, LLC.

Published by Tate Publishing & Enterprises, LLC
127 E. Trade Center Terrace | Mustang, Oklahoma 73064 USA
1.888.361.9473 | www.tatepublishing.com

Tate Publishing is committed to excellence in the publishing industry. The company reflects the philosophy established by the founders, based on Psalm 68:11,
"The Lord gave the word and great was the company of those who published it."

Book design copyright © 2016 by Tate Publishing, LLC. All rights reserved.
Cover design by Ray Costa and Norlan Balazo
Interior design by Mary Jean Archival

Published in the United States of America

ISBN: 978-1-68187-897-3
Biography & Autobiography / Sports
16.09.16

ACKNOWLEDGMENTS

I'd like to share my sincere gratitude to Mike London and the entire London family for giving me the opportunity to bring Danny London back to life.

COVER DESIGN
by
Ray Costa
CopyLine@aol.com

FOREWORD

My career in sports writing has allowed me to enter many arenas, coliseums and playing fields. I have witnessed many miracles in these venues. The story of Danny London's miracle and his boxing phenomenon that gave him a second chance to be the champion featherweight is a one of a kind story. His story is one that should be read by sports fans and anyone interested in a man's struggle to achieve his life's dream.

—Nathan Gottlieb, HBO boxing writer and author

1

My father looked into my eyes and tried to make me understand what he was saying to me. It wasn't clear. Again, I couldn't comprehend his meaning. He looked in the direction of my mother as I watched his lips move and felt the vibrations of his words. My mother left the kitchen and returned with a clean white shirt that she dressed me up with, and put a small blue necktie on me. My mother gave me a gentle hug. My father took my hand and led me out the door of our sixth floor apartment, which was the top floor of the apartment building where we lived in on Pitt Street in Brooklyn, New York, USA.

I was born in 1914 on the crowded lower east side of New York City. My mother was sick and lost her hearing when I was born. I was born deaf and mute. It took my parents more than a year to realize that I couldn't hear or speak. The doctor they brought me to was the best in the city of that era. His examination indicated that I had a dead nerve behind my right ear, which caused my inability to speak and hear.

Despite this rough start in my life, here I was in front of the whole world. Me, couldn't talk, couldn't hear. Here

John J. Morabito

I am. Now, within the surrounding ropes, seeing two fists flying at my face in a duel that may someday decide my chance to fight for the featherweight championship of the world! How did this happen? How could I even believe that such a miracle of change would ever happen, especially to me? This is my story.

I was just turning seven years old as my father held my hand leaving our sixth story walk-up to enter the street. The neighborhood kids were playing in the park across the street from my building. There were many ethnic families in our neighborhood, such as Polish, Greek, Italian, Hungarian, German, and Irish. My family was Jewish. I was always embarrassed by the way the kids pointed at me and made strange faces. I was different and out of place at seven years old. I felt alone.

My father's tight grip on my hand made me feel safe, yet I could also feel the vibrations of his many unspoken frustrations of raising a family as large as ours. My mother gave birth to eleven kids. I had five brothers: Jack, Sammy, Hymie, Eddie, and Willie; and four sisters: Marylyn, Shirley, Esther, and Annie. As I was, I felt like I was the burden of the brood. I also sensed anger through my father's hand, anger created from my curious stupid mistakes. I remember when I was trying to help out at his cigar-making store, somewhere near Bowling Green, where he employed five people including my brothers, Eddie and Sammy. We would tear down the tobacco leaves and roll them up and put them in a damp case. He would make the best handmade cigars around. One day I stole an expensive Cuban cigar and went into the cellar and tried to smoke it. The smoke became extremely heavy and rose into the store. My father called the fire department. They arrived only to find me sick and dizzy with the cigar in my hand. The fireman said, "You smoke cigars?" I still feel the stinging on my butt from the spanking my father gave me.

My father took me to a sign reading school, which I was approved for from the interview I had the previous month. It was not far from our Pitt Street apartment. He and my mother knew it was time for me to become educated so that I could communicate, and signing and lip reading was what I needed to learn.

2

Miss Kearns, the principal, explained to my father that I was accepted and that there was an adult in the school that would escort me home after school each day. My father was grateful for the offer. My father gave me a kiss on the forehead and a warm hug. Moving his lips slowly, he said a clear "Behave." After he left, Miss Kearns led me down the corridor to classroom 5B.

Miss Kearns tapped lightly on the door and it opened showing an extremely huge woman about six feet tall with broad shoulders blocking the entrance. Miss Kearns introduced me, "This is David London, your new student." The teacher bent over and put her face to mine to make sure I watched her lips move and answered, "I'm Miss Sheffield." Miss Kearns left and Miss Sheffield led me into the room of many deaf and mute students.

I was shy and felt embarrassed as I entered. They were all looking at me with wide eyes when Miss Sheffield raised her hands and started to sign, telling the students my name and that I would be attending the school in class 5B with them.

The kids in the class were all being taught lip reading, but whenever Miss Sheffield left the room the kids would begin signing. When she returned and caught any one signing when they should be lip reading she would punish them by making them stay after school and continue to lip read. I was having a difficult time learning lip reading and signing and it was apparent that Miss Sheffield was getting very frustrated with me.

There were two flashing lights on the wall; one was yellow and one green. The yellow light flashed for a few seconds to inform all the students that it was lunchtime. The green flashed at the end of the school day and it was time to go home.

The yellow light flashed and I followed the class to the lunchroom. I sat alone eating my lunch when a pretty girl with red hair from another class stood in front of me and started to sign. I was blushing and then turned completely red with embarrassment. It took me a couple of days to find out that she was asking me my name, and when I finally understood, I walked up to her and signed my name, David London, and she signed Harriet. She handed me the alphabet sign language paper and I took it home and studied it every night and Harriet helped me at school every day. It took me about two months to finally understand how to sign.

I became best friends with Harriet. I went to the candy store and bought her a ring for two cents. I gave it to her and signed, "Thank you for helping me." Harriet kissed my cheek and I felt so good. As time went by I became pretty proficient at signing.

My mother always made me leave the room whenever I was practicing signing and told me to go to the cellar where it was musty and smelly. I never understood why she acted this way. This made me mad, but I couldn't yell out at her.

When I was almost ten years old, on the weekends I went to the playground across the street with my friend, Mutty, who lived in the apartment on the fifth floor in my building. I let him straddle my shoulders and I carried him up to his apartment. I was becoming physically strong.

3

Walking around Brooklyn I saw many boys from the neighborhood on the corners with shoe shine boxes. I clearly noticed they were making money. It was hard times in the city and they needed to help out their families any way they could, and I realized I needed to do the same.

I went into the cellar and made a shine box, it came out perfect. I showed it to my mother and she said, "You're very handy, David, what are you going to do with it?" I told her that I would shine shoes on the corner and make some money to help support her. "Go ahead and make some money and bring it to me."

I went out on the street. With my shine box slung across my shoulder, I tried to find an unoccupied street corner, but most were already taken. As I walked, I was getting dirty looks and vulgar gestures from the shine boys. Finally, I found an empty corner and set down my shine box.

My first customer came and put his shoe on my box. I felt nervous, knowing that I never shined anyone's shoes before. I put polish on his shoe and started brushing when he became upset and angrily asked why I didn't wash his shoe first. I didn't understand. I couldn't make out what he was saying. I felt so embarrassed, because I had no idea what he was saying or what I did wrong. All the other shine boys were now looking at me making faces and yelling words that I couldn't make out. I was mad and I tried to tell the customer that I would redo his shoes. I put some oil on his shoes and he became irate and started yelling for the police. I took my shine box and ran home. I hid in the cellar for a long time shaking.

When I entered my apartment I observed my mother crudely signing in Jewish with her index finger and thumb, "Mach Gelt? Mach Gelt?" It was hard at first for me to understand until I realized she was asking me about the money I made.

I said that the corners were filled with too many shine boys and not enough customers. She looked at me with doubtful eyes and I looked back at her with determined eyes saying I would make some money shining shoes.

Secretly, while making believe I was playing, I watched the more seasoned shine boys from the park to see how they worked their customers. I then bought the shoe wash and correct polish. The next day as I passed the other shine boys, they called me names. I felt the vibrations of their voices. They were Jew haters, yelling, "Go home, you Jew bastard." It didn't matter, because I was back on my corner ready for business.

I motioned with my hands and lips telling them, "No, I'll stay right here."

One of the taller boys, a Polish kid by the name of Mike, came over to the corner and told me, "Leave and go home, you Jew son-of-a-bitch."

I motioned with my fingers and lips, "I stay right here."

Mike shoved and pushed my shoulders, I pushed him back, he pushed me again and I jabbed him and hit him with a right cross. He went down on the sidewalk with his nose bleeding. The other boys turned away like little lambs. From that moment on they were my friends and this was my corner. Then I realized I could throw a damn good punch.

Mutty, my good friend, and I would play at the park and go to many different areas of the city. Through signing and lip reading, he explained what people were talking about. He was a true friend.

School was not easy. My ability to sign and lip-read improved, but my relationship with the monster Miss Sheffield grew so sour that each and every day became unbearable.

I returned to school each Monday, and each time I was continually reprimanded for one thing or another, like signing and lip reading with other students when I needed to pay attention to Miss Sheffield. For some reason she really had it out for me.

Miss Sheffield always carried a pointer stick that she tapped on a desk or a chair when she wanted the attention of the class. The vibrations would get more and more intense when the students didn't respond immediately. I was talking for a second to my friend, Salvatore, when Miss Sheffield came over to me. She started whipping me with the pointer. It stung so bad that tears began to well up in my eyes. Finally when I had enough I stood up, grabbed the stick from her hand, and broke it over my knee. Then without thinking I threw the pieces in her face and ran out of the room and left the building.

The next morning I returned to school and all the kids were smiling and winking at me. They were glad for what I did to Miss Sheffield. When Miss Sheffield entered the room, I noticed she had a Band Aid across her nose. She approached me and grasped my arm, lifted me out of my seat, and told me to go to the principal's office to see Miss Kearns.

I sat for a long while in the principal's office when Miss Kearns motioned me to come in. She was angry and upset, and told me that I was expelled and not allowed back at school. I pretended I was sad, but inside I was grinning, I didn't like Miss Sheffield and signing school was boring.

The next few days I waited for the mailman to come, because I was sure there would be a letter to my parents about my behavior and the reason for my expulsion. My thought was right. The mail came and there was a letter from the school. I read and understood that they didn't want me there anymore. I took it into the cellar, took a book of matches out of my pocket and burned it. Now my parents would never know about the letter or what it said.

4

I was feeling lost and didn't know what to do with myself. My parents were sure I was in school each day, learning and doing well. I had to find a job, a job that would allow me to be home each day by three o'clock so that I could continue to pretend that I was still attending signing school.

I needed to make myself look a little older. I put on a heavy flannel shirt, a leather jacket, and a cap. My mother said that I was supposed to be wearing a white shirt and tie to school, but I told her that it was cool outside and that I liked walking to school instead of taking the subway.

I felt so guilty for lying, but my choices were limited to either letting them know the truth or getting through this time of my life by myself and paying the price at a later date.

I left my apartment and walked down to Canal Street looking for any opportunity to get work and make some money. The entire city was struggling to survive and I was just one of many looking for a job.

I met a friend, Casey, from my neighborhood, and he knew my handicap and the basics of signing. I asked him if there were any jobs where he was working. He told me that his boss was looking for a delivery boy part time and gave me his name and address. I thanked him and went to look for his boss.

Eventually, I located the address and the boss off of Canal Street. He was tall and strictly business with a stern face. He looked me over for a couple of minutes and then asked me my name. He realized then that I had a handicap and asked me my age. I lied and told him I was fifteen years old. He asked me if I knew the city. I assured him that I was familiar with all areas of the city. He said that the job consisted of delivering fabric uptown, east and west around the city. The pay was twenty- five cents an hour. I accepted and began working the same day. I carried the fabric rolls on my shoulder to the addresses my boss gave me. The vibrations of the cars, trucks, busses, and subways ran through me. The vibrations of mumbled voices of the people going about their business became a part of me.

The job worked out perfectly for my schedule. I was responsible to make deliveries twice a day, which allowed me to be home by three. I earned about ten dollars a week for deliveries. On the weekends I shined shoes and now had many customers.

I shined shoes for a nickel. If I did a good job I would get a tip of a nickel. At the end of the day I made three or four dollars. I'd give the money to my mother who would give me twenty-five cents for pocket change. That didn't sit too well with me, but that was the way it was.

One day I left the house early so my mother wouldn't see me with my shine box. I shined all day and made seventy-five cents. I entered my apartment and went directly to the bathroom on the top floor and hid the seventy-five behind the toilet. I was in my room lying down when my mother entered and signed that she found seventy-five cents behind the toilet on the top floor. I felt myself getting flushed in the face, but I just smiled even though I was mad as hell inside. "You're very lucky," I signed with a wink.

5

My parents kissed me on the cheek each morning, thinking I was going to school, but I was now approaching twelve years old and my job sometimes kept me later in the afternoon making deliveries. My parents were concerned with my lateness from school so many days during the week.

It was time to confess and I told them the entire story, the truth about what happened with Miss Sheffield. To my surprise, they stuck up for me and both gave me a hug. "What will you do with yourself, David?" my father asked.

My signing was now perfect and he clearly understood my answer. "I will shine shoes, that's all, and I won't deliver any fabric anymore." My parents seemed content with my decision and the next day I found my spot on the corner of Pitt Street and all my customers became regulars.

Life on the corner shining shoes at twelve years old was not too bad. I was making money, bringing it home to my mother and that made her happy. I was now an ace at shining and the following of my customers grew and they were faithful.

I was in the middle of shining a customer's shoes once when a big, six-foot Irish cop began chasing the shine boys off the corners. He stood over me until I finished the customer's shoes and then bellowed, "Stay off this corner, I'm warning you, don't come back here." I nodded okay and left the corner. An hour later I was back on the corner along with the other shine boys. In the middle of shinning a customer's shoes, I saw all the shine boys pick up their boxes and run, the big blow hard Irish cop was back. No one thought he'd return. I was stuck. I couldn't run because I had to finish the customer's shoes. He screamed and cursed at me. He grabbed my shine box and threw it into the street where it shattered into a million pieces.

I was furious. I was so mad I kicked his ankle hard and ran. He flung his nightstick at me and hit me hard on my ass. That hurt so badly. I ran all the way back home and into the cellar and stayed there for an hour. When I came out, I looked around and the big son-of-a-bitch Irish cop was gone.

The next few days, me, Mutty, and Frankie, one of the shine boys, loaded our pockets with onions that we bought from the local produce store. We went up on the roof of our building and waited for that lousy bastard to come by. He didn't come by that day. We waited the second day for two hours and then Frankie spotted him, "There he is!" We threw onions at his giant head and just missed it by a hair; he ducked in the doorway of a store and we ran, jumping from rooftop to rooftop. He never found out who threw the onions.

The cops were now continually on the corners and we shine boys had to give up our work on the corner of Pitt Street. I was lost for work; there was nothing around. I found a job uptown on Thirty-ninth Street and Eighth Avenue shining shoes in a boot black parlor. I made ten dollars a week with tips, but after a couple of months I quit. My mother called me dirty names and pinched me on my arm every chance she got.

The next day my mom asked where I was going.

"I'm going to look for a new job, one that will pay more." I went downtown and was just kind of bumming around when I stumbled upon a sign on the wall of a building. "Boxer Training 12 p.m. to 3 p.m., 6 p.m. to 9 p.m." It was 1 p.m., so I went upstairs and paid the ten-cent entry fee to watch the fighters train. It was a dump, a smelly, sweat-soaked place, but the fighters were pros—Sid Terris, Ruby Goldstein, Charlie Rosenberg, and Al Singer. The training caught my interest and I stayed there all day watching the boxers train.

One of the fighters stopped to talk to a big shot dressed in a suit and wearing a white fedora smoking a fat cigar. The boxer's face was rugged, his nose was flat and his left ear had a big lump on it, known as a cauliflower ear. As he passed by me he looked at me and winked. At that moment I knew I wanted a cauliflower ear. I wanted people to know that I was a fighter.

On my way home to have supper with my family, I couldn't get the image of the boxer and the gym out of my thoughts. I continually played the training bouts over and over in my mind. I wanted to learn more about the boxers and the art of boxing, but I was only twelve years old.

The whole family was at the dinner table except for my older brother, Willie. He was a Merchant Marine and was at sea. Sammy and Eddie were jazz musicians. Sammy played the trumpet and Eddie played the trombone. I couldn't hear the music, but the vibration of their instruments was soothing. My mother always prepared a fine meal and my sisters always cleared the table and did the dishes. I left the table after dinner and went to my room and began to shadow box.

My moves were crude as I was trying to imitate the fighters at the gym, throwing jabs with my left hand and crosses with my right. My mom came in the room.

"Are you planning to fight someone, David?"

I told her that I was just practicing to protect myself because so many guys in the neighborhood start trouble with me.

My mom left the bedroom and went back to the kitchen where she told the rest of the family that I was acting crazy.

"I think he's trying to find out what he wants to be."

Annie looked up from the table.

"He wants to be a fighter, a boxer?"

I was nearly thirteen years old and to my surprise I found a gym across the street from my apartment building not far from the park. It wasn't much of a gym, a couple of pugs training, skipping rope and exercising on a floor mat. There weren't any punching bags, no boxing ring, just a circle on the floor where guys would spar.

I made it a habit of going there each night to watch the pugs train and work out. I didn't care what anybody thought or said to me. I was doing what I wanted to do, learning how to box.

I became a regular at the gym and befriended a boxing trainer, Mickey, who signed me, asking if I would like to go to Stillman's Gym uptown on Eighth Avenue where all the greats trained. I motioned to him that I would very much like to go there with him. Mickey paid for my fare on the subway. We got off uptown and walked to the gym. This was such a great experience for me. My eyes lit up and almost bugged out of my head when I walked in. It cost twenty-five cents to enter, but it was well worth every penny.

Jack Dempsey, Primo Carnera, Jack Sharkey, Tommy Loughran were training there. I was shy and nervous and turned away when Jack Sharkey looked at me and winked. Gene Tunney would not train at Stillman's with the closed windows. Because of the odors and unsanitary conditions, he refused to go in, and the management refused to open the windows.

This was a real gym. There were two boxing rings and always fighters sitting on a bench waiting their turn to spar in the ring, Upstairs there were six heavy bags, five speed bags, and jumping ropes hanging on the wall. I thought someday when I become a great boxer this is where I'll train.

6

Time moved on and when I was almost fourteen years old I started training at a better gym on Pitt Street. It wasn't anything like Stillman's, but it was close to my apartment. Anyhow, they would never let a young nobody like me train at Stillman's. I was shadow boxing at Pitt Street Gym as a stranger continued to watch me. After awhile he approached me speaking and I read his lips. "You shadow box just like Tommy Loughran." Tommy Loughran was the light-heavy weight champion of the world at this time.

The man asked me my age.

Using hand gestures and slowly mouthing the words, I was able to answer all of his questions and he understood. He realized I was deaf and mute.

"Fourteen."

"How much do you weigh?"

"Ninety-five pounds."

"You're too young and too light, you'll need to wait two more years."

I felt depressed and discouraged. I wanted to box, I didn't want to wait any longer.

"What's your name?"

"David."

"David, you can come to this gym anytime you want, you're welcome here."

I felt a little better because he seemed interested in me and was willing to take the time to actually communicate with me.

"My name is Doc Reiner."

He had a pencil thin moustache and high cheekbones. He wore a short brimmed straw hat cocked to one side of his head. He wrote his name on a piece of paper and handed it to me. *I'm a trainer and if you come here I'll teach you how to box.*

I felt alive, my mood uplifted. Doc Reiner appeared to be well respected in the gym and knowledgeable about boxing. I came to the gym every day after meeting Doc Reiner, and he lived up to his statement of teaching me how to train and box.

I learned how to shadow box and skip rope. He taught me a routine of exercises to get into shape. I was faithful to my training schedule and never missed a day. After months of training with Doc I entered the gym when he was talking to a boxer. The boxer walked over to me and using crude signing asked me if I wanted to box a couple of rounds.

"Yes, sure, sure," I signed.

Doc Reiner put the gloves on me and made me face him directly so I was able to read his lips.

"I don't want you to do anything but jab, jab, jab, and right cross, understand?"

I tried to understand what Doc Reiner said and after several repeats I thought I understood his directions. I also had to be aware of when he called time by looking over at his lips. I came out slugging toward this guy with a flat nose. All I wanted him to do was hit me in the ear. I wanted a cauliflower ear, the mark of a genuine fighter in my eyes. I wanted people to know I was a fighter and gain their respect, but this guy was slugging at me too, and he missed too many punches and never hit my ear.

When I looked over at Doc his face looked extremely mad.

"Time. Time. I don't want you to do any infighting, just jab, jab, and right cross."

Still it was difficult for me to understand his instructions. The next round I came out slugging, I didn't jab or throw any right crosses.

"TIME!"

Doc Reiner took my gloves off and wrote on a piece of paper and handed it to me. *Go home and then go find yourself a job as a bootblack.*

I threw the note at him and walked out of the gym totally livid and disgusted. All my training and hard work were for nothing. I was so frustrated with myself. I couldn't get the instructions Doc Reiner was trying to get across to me. I had to find a way to understand what Doc was instructing me to do.

The year was 1926. My good friend Mutty and I went to the movies in Times Square to see the great Jack Dempsey's fight against Gene Tunney for the heavyweight championship of the world. I watched how Dempsey fought. He was rough and tough, slugging all his punches. Tunney was a master, classy and smart, just jabbing Dempsey throughout the fight. A light bulb went off in my head. I knew what Doc Reiner was trying to teach me. I would strive to do better the next time I fought.

I became friends with an amateur boxer I met at the gym, featherweight and Kings County Champion Al Peters. He had it all as a strong, well-conditioned Polish kid. He was a snappy fast boxer. I carried his valise so I could get into the amateur bouts. There were ten bouts in the amateur contest and Al Peters was in the final bout. He won in the third round and received a large diamond ring.

I was thrilled to be with Al. We became good friends, he became pretty efficient at talking slowly to me so I could understand him and he was able to read my lips and understand some hand gestures. I ran a lot of errands for him. I had dinner at his house and sometimes he'd ask me to sleep over. Al Peters knew that I wanted to become an amateur boxer, so I asked him about getting my amateur card.

"Do you know where the Woolworth Building is uptown?"

"Yes." I nodded.

"Go there and ask Ben Levine for an application for an amateur card, it costs twenty-five cents."

I thanked Al for the information.

The next morning I dressed in the outfit that I felt made me look older—a heavy flannel shirt, leather coat with my cap turned up. I found the Woolworth Building and Ben Levine's office and asked him for the application for an amateur card. Ben Levine was a nice man, unassuming and helpful. He took his time with me and showed me how to complete the application and then asked for the twenty-five-cent fee.

I filled out the application easily. I thought there's nothing to this and returned it to Ben Levine. He asked

Danny London

my age and I began to breathe hard and perspire. I had to lie to him, I wrote down sixteen.

"Okay, then take this application to your parents and have them sign it and return it."

I nodded in agreement. Now what was I to do? I wanted to be an amateur fighter. I wanted to box. It meant a lot to me but I knew that my parents would never sign knowing I was fourteen years old. It took me a long time to think this situation through.

I went back home to find Mutty. I was sure he would help me with my plan.

I met Mutty outside of the building and asked him if he would ask his parents to sign my application.

"Application for what?" Mutty asked.

"For my amateur card for boxing."

"Come to my apartment after dinner tonight."

I finished dinner with my family and went into my room to get the application, then I left the apartment and went down stairs to Mutty's apartment. His parents were always kind to me, and Mutty had already explained to them my situation. Mutty's parents looked over the application and had a question for me.

"David, on the application your name states that you're Danny London, not David. Did you make a mistake?"

"No, I'll fight under the name Danny London just in case I win a fight and it gets in the newspaper. I don't want my parents to know it's me."

They both roared with laughter and signed the application and handed it to me.

"Please don't get hurt in the ring," Mutty's parents stressed.

"Please, don't worry, I fight in the streets every day against kids that pick on me, but now I'll fight in the ring and keep out of trouble on the streets. I want to win prizes and money and some day turn professional."

The next day I woke early because I couldn't wait to get to the Woolworth Building and go into Ben Levine's office to get my Amateur Boxing card. I walked slowly uptown and was the first one in Ben Levine's office. He reviewed the application.

"Good luck, Danny London."

My card was handed to me and in bold letters, "Danny London" was printed on the front. I left the building and put my hands in my pockets and strolled down the avenue. I was elated and tried to whistle but nothing came out. As I approached the apartment building I met Mutty and reminded him that my amateur card was a secret. He shook my hand and wished me good luck.

The next day I went to the five and dime store and bought fifteen cents' worth of clay. I brought it home, went into my bedroom, and locked the door. I took the clay from the bag and began shaping it into an ear, a cauliflower ear, but my skills with clay were not good and it looked more like a potato than a cauliflower. However, I molded it onto my left ear and pressed it very hard so it would stay on. I looked in the mirror and agreed with myself that it didn't look too bad, so I left the apartment with the piece of clay on my ear and strolled down the busy street. People looked at me and stared and I believed that they knew I was a fighter. But then the sun got hot and the clay fell off my ear and I kicked it into the street.

A few days later I was walking on Delancey Street and ran into Doc Reiner. I quickly showed him my amateur card. Going back and forth lip reading we had a conversation.

"Did you change your name?"

"Yes, my name is Danny London now."

"Do you want to box in an exhibition bout?"

"Yes, when and where?"

"Come down to the Pitt Street Park Gym at eight o'clock tomorrow night."

"Will I get anything if I win?"

"No, because it's an exhibition bout, but you'll get experience and that's what you need, Danny."

Doc Reiner knew I needed to get better and he was a good trainer and teacher. I would now work hard to try and understand him.

7

My mind was racing. A real exhibition bout. This was what I wanted, and now I have what I asked for—a chance to fight!

I stayed in my bedroom with the door closed. I did push-ups and shadow boxed and more push-ups and shadow boxing until the door opened and my older brother Jack was standing in the doorway watching me shadow boxing. I told Jack the whole story and showed him my card. I pleaded with him not to tell our parents. I really didn't know if I could trust him, but I took a chance.

The next day was dragging on like watching paint dry, but I kept myself busy by exercising and jabbing with my left and throwing right crosses. I thought of Gene Tunney and what Doc Reiner tried to drill into my head about boxing, not slugging.

It was getting close to seven o'clock, so I left the apartment and started walking to the Pitt Street Gym. I didn't have any gear, just a pair of training trunks. When I entered the gym I saw more than a hundred people in attendance. A nervous feeling started to overwhelm me. I saw Doc Reiner waving to me and motioning me to come over. I followed him into the dressing room and he gave me a pair of boxing shoes, taped up my hands, and put the gloves on me. I still didn't know whom I was fighting.

Doc Reiner said that it was time to go to the ring. We left the dressing room and as I walked toward the ring I felt the mumbling vibrations from the tremendous crowd. When we reached the ring he lifted the ropes and I jumped up. I gasped, when to my surprise standing in the opposite corner was Al Peters. Al Peters weighed 118 pounds and I weighted only 98 pounds. What the hell was Doc Reiner thinking? What did he get me into? I knew at that moment Al Peters was an excellent boxer with experience.

When the first round bell rung, I felt the vibrations and saw the lips of the referee mouth "TIME." Al Peters had the eyes of a fighter, one who keeps his eyes focused on his opponent's gloves, never looking in my eyes. He outjabbed me in the first round, and the second round was the same. I was outjabbed. All I wanted him to do was hit me in the ear. I longed for a cauliflower ear because then everyone would know I was a fighter. As I sat on the corner stool, Doc Reiner motioned me to jab, jab. I shook my head in agreement.

The third round bell rung. My patience and plan of throwing jabs disappeared. I came out slugging. I was throwing my right hand like a crazy man and caught Al Peters above his left eye and left a half-inch cut. It was bleeding profusely so the fight was stopped. I was scared and worried when I went to Al's corner and apologized. I told him I never meant to do that. Al looked me straight in the face and slowly mouthed these words.

"Don't worry, Danny, it's a small cut that will heal fast."

He shook my hand with a strong grip and we remained good friends.

Doc Reiner took me to the dressing room and praised me for being a strong opponent. He knew that Al Peters outweighed me and had more experience.

"You fought a good fight, Danny."

I left the gym and walked outside and to my surprise my mother was standing there waiting for me. The look in her eyes was colder than the look in Al Peters' eyes. I was positive that Jack told her everything and it was time for me to come clean. I knew there was no explanation my mother would accept.

She grabbed my ear and pulled me all the way home calling me several obscene names. If I was ever to get a cauliflower ear it wasn't going to be in the ring, it was going to come from my mother. When we got to the apartment, she went to her room and I went to mine and immediately went to sleep.

The next morning I woke and had some breakfast. My mother came in and I told her that I was going out to look for a job. She smiled and didn't call me any names or make any terrible hand gestures so I left and went directly to Stillman's Gym. I stayed there all day watching the seasoned fighters train. I wanted to learn the tricks and techniques of the trade used to fight their opponents.

I got home late that day and I told mom I didn't feel well and went to my bedroom. I looked in the mirror and began shadow boxing. The door suddenly opened and my mother stood in the doorway.

"I thought you were sick, you big faker."

"Well, I feel a little better now."

I lay down for a while before supper with the family. I had visions of me someday fighting for a big payday.

My father came from work and the family sat down for dinner. He looked over at me with a disgusted look on his face and began signing.

"All you do is bum around all day. You're not being a good boy."

I couldn't answer him. My mind was on fire with madness and everyone at the table seemed to be against me.

I was nearing fifteen years old and my goal was to stay focused and continue training and learning the true art of boxing. A few days had passed and I went to the gym on Pitt Street and met Al Peters. His eye was nearly healed and he was cordial to me.

Al pulled me aside and moved his lips slowly so that I could understand what he was saying.

"Danny, you're an excellent boxer. You'll make a good amateur. Keep training hard and it will soon pay off."

It was so great to hear positive compliments from a boxer of Peters' status. He was always truthful with me and I felt the positive vibrations from him.

I told him that my parents were against me boxing and they continued to verbally beat me up.

"Don't you worry about them. You make up a good alibi and it'll be fine."

"I've lied to them too many times already. What else can I say to them? When will you fight again?"

"Next week, Friday night at Saint Anthony's Church Arena."

"Can I carry your bag and be your lowboy?"

"Sure you can, Danny. Be at my house Friday night at six and we'll go to the arena together."

Danny London

I trained all week long at the Pitt Street Gym and when Friday came I took the day off and rested. I went to Al's house where there was a car waiting to take him to the arena. I sat next to him in the back seat feeling like royalty.

We got to the arena and went to the dressing room where Doc Reiner and his partner, Jimmy Fazio, were waiting to work in Al's corner. I felt terrific being a part of the whole scene. A rumor was spreading that all the boxers on the bill showed tonight but one in the flyweight division was a no show.

Al heard about the problem and confronted Doc Reiner.

"Why can't we put Danny in the bout? He has his amateur card."

Doc Reiner knows that I'm way too light to fight in this class. But he thinks for a bit and comes over to me.

"Danny, go outside and find some stones and load your pockets up with them. Make it fast."

I ran around the arena in circles picking up all the small stones I could find. I went back into the dressing room looking like I just crapped my pants. Doc Reiner looked at me with a boyish grin.

"You did all right. Now take off your shirt and shoes and leave your pants on."

We went to the scale to weigh in and to my surprise I went from 98 pounds to 113 pounds. I just gained 15 pounds. Al Peters was always thinking of me. He gave me his boxing gear to use before his main event bout. Al put his hand on my shoulder so that I would give him my full attention. He slowly moved his lips to let me know that this guy could box and he had a sneaky right hand.

Doc Reiner put the gloves on me and looked me in the eyes.

"Remember to jab, jab. Keep jabbing a lot."

Doc Reiner and I made our way from the dressing room to the ring and climbed into the ring together. The arena was filled to capacity with fans and spectators and press. I felt the tumultuous vibrations of the crowd. I sat down on the corner stool and looked at the middle of the mat that was covered with bloodstains that scared me to death.

My opponent climbed into the ring. He was wearing a robe marked with his name on the back: K. O. AL WEIN.

I looked at him and shivered as Doc and I went to the center of the ring for the referee's instructions.

"This is a three-round bout."

Doc Reiner told the referee that I couldn't hear the bell.

"That's okay, I'll take care of him. When the bell rings, I'll stop him and send him to his corner."

The bell rang and I felt the vibrations. I hope he tags my ear so I can get a cauliflower ear and people will know I am a serious fighter.

I outboxed him in rounds one, two, and three. He never touched my ear because I ducked all of his punches. To my amazement I won my very first fight and received a wristwatch for first prize.

I went back to the dressing room where Al put his arm around my shoulder.

"Congratulations, Danny."

"Thanks, Al. I hope you win your bout too."

Doc came face to face with me and slowly spoke. "You're improving your jabs and right cross punches. You really surprised me, but you must continue to practice the left jab. It's the bread and butter punch."

Al Peters fought the main event and won the decision. He received the same prize for first place, a wristwatch. We left the arena and there were many people mulling around. A stranger approached us and asked if we would like to sell our watches for ten dollars apiece. We agreed and took the money. We went to a fabulous restaurant and ate a fine meal. I got home late that night and my mother was waiting up for me. She was worried and looked aggravated, but before she had a chance to call me names I gave her five dollars.

"Where did you get the money?"

"I fought my first amateur bout and won a wristwatch that I sold for ten dollars."

"Where is the other five dollars? Too much money for you to carry."

"I went to a restaurant and ate."

"Why are you fighting amateur fights?"

"Mom, I'm fighting for my future, I'm fighting for our future. I want to fight for the championship one day."

"You better go to bed before your Dad beats you up."

"I want you to tell Dad everything. It's important to me that you both know that this is what I want to do. I'm learning to be a boxer. It's not just fighting, it's a business and there's a future in it for me."

My mom's expression surprised me. She understood my signing as she looked at me with pride. I was more than just a young kid wasting his time fooling around in a gym. I was going to be a boxer and there was acceptance in her face. She kissed me good night and I went to bed.

8

The next day I went to the newsstand and bought a copy of the *Brooklyn Eagle* newspaper. I turned to the sports page and found the fight results. There was the article on the fight, it was as tiny as dictionary print, but it was all there.

> Danny London outslings Al Wein in three rounds and wins in the fly weight division.

I was so proud of myself and wanted to share my win, so as I walked everyone I met I would let them read the article. I wanted to box more and win and definitely become well known in the fight game.

I headed toward the Pitt Street Gym and on my way I met Doc Reiner. He came right up to me and put his arm around my shoulder, then he looked at me.

"Danny, take a break from training today and come to Stillman's Gym with me."

"Sure, Doc. Maybe I can watch and learn more from the fighters there and get better."

"That's it, Danny. Now you're thinking like a winner."

So we went to Stillman's and Doc was friendly with all the boxers. He knew so many people there. He introduced me to them all and I felt good.

After watching all the boxers train, we headed back home. I turned toward Doc to get his attention.

"When will I fight again?"

"Right now you're too light to fight and we can't continue to load your pockets with stones. I want you to start eating lots of potatoes, bread, steak, and vegetables and gain some weight."

"Okay, Doc, that's what I'll do."

Food like that was rare around the kitchen of our struggling family, but I knew I needed to follow Doc's instructions.

I went back to work as a bootblack to earn some extra cash. I worked in a shoeshine parlor on Delancey Street every weekend and in three days I made ten dollars. I made it a part of my routine to stop at the produce market and buy potatoes and vegetables, and go to the butcher shop and buy Porterhouse steak so that my mother could cook it for me and the rest of the family.

I was there for three months, saved fifty dollars' worth of tips and continued to give my mother ten dollars a week to help support her.

She wasn't aware that I had saved fifty dollars otherwise she would have snatched it from me too. I went searching for Doc Reiner at the candy store on Pitt Street where he always hung out. There he was standing outside the door.

"Doc, I have fifty dollars and I want you to help me buy some boxing equipment."

Doc's eyes lit up and he looked at me with the knowledge of how serious I was about being a well-trained boxer. He and I both knew after my last fight and win that I was maturing and improving my skills.

Doc Reiner brought me to the Everlast Sports Equipment Factory located somewhere north of Manhattan, possibly in the Bronx. I never was in this neighborhood but Doc Reiner knew where to get all the right equipment at the right price.

I bought boxing shoes, trunks, protector cup, head guard, and two pairs of boxing gloves, all for forty dollars. The prices in the factory were cheap, and after all my purchases I had ten dollars left.

"Doc, let me take you to a fine Jewish restaurant. I want to thank you for your help."

Doc Reiner and I sat in a popular restaurant on Suffolk Street and had the biggest steak on the menu. It was hearty and our bellies were full to the top when we left. As we walked by a local drug store Doc Reiner suggested we go in and weigh me on their scale.

I stepped on the scale, and it shot up to 108 pounds.

"Not bad. Now you don't have to put so many stones in your pockets." We both laughed till our sides hurt.

"Where am I going to put all this boxing equipment? I can't bring it home. I don't want my parents to know I bought it all."

"Just tell them I gave it to you as a present."

"No, Doc, that won't work. They would never believe me."

"Okay then, I'll bring it all to Al Peters' house. He'll let you store it there and you can get it whenever you want."

I was still only fourteen years old when Doc took me to Willie Beecher's Gym in Brownsville, Brooklyn. The gym was a sweaty smelly place, but there was a boxing ring, heavy bag, weight pulleys, and mats for exercising. Beecher's was as big as Stillman's. But you had to be a professional to train at Stillman's.

I began going to Beecher's every day. I was getting in great shape, getting stronger and gaining weight. Doc worked with me every day and continued to show me how important it was to jab and use the right cross. Doc began to see a change in me as I obeyed his instructions and directions in and out of the ring. I knew it was hard for him to sometimes communicate with me, but he was relentless in making me understand what he wanted me to do.

The training and workouts at Beecher's went so well and Doc put me in boxing exhibition bouts for a while. I did fairly well in the bouts, so Doc decided to get me into the Kings County Amateur Championship.

It was spring 1929. I was fifteen years old and my skills had improved. I won seven fights in a row with four fights left. I had to win them all.

I won the next three fights. The fourth fight came down to Al Howard, a more experienced fighter, and me. I lost. I received a silver medal. I was so discouraged and came down on myself hard. I really wanted the title.

Doc sensed how discouraged I felt and tried to help me out.

"Danny, I want you to take a month off and rest, you worked hard and I don't want you to burn out. Don't worry, you'll have the championship one day."

"I hope so, Doc."

I went home and told my father about the fight, and he amazed me with his words of encouragement. "Keep up the good work, David. Someday you'll be the champion."

"I feel like I could fight tomorrow for the title. I have so much confidence now."

"Take it easy, have patience, don't rush."

I went to him and kissed him on the cheek. "I'll do better next time."

After a month of rest, I was back training at Beecher's Gym. Everybody knew me now. I was becoming well known in the gym. It felt great. I had two weeks to train and get ready for the amateur bouts. I trained hard and stayed in excellent condition.

9

I trained for two solid weeks when Doc took me to Saint Anthony's Church Club. The arena was decent and they had a dressing room with a shower and plenty of hot water. We went to the dressing room and Doc told me to take off everything but my pants. He moved his lips slowly so I could understand.

"Leave them on."

When we came out the dressing room about thirty amateur boxers were standing there ready to weigh in. I had listened to Doc and changed my diet to gain weight. I now weighed 116 pounds. When it was my turn to get on the scale, Doc was right behind me. I stepped on the scale and I felt a hand under my butt lifting me up. I weighed in at 112 pounds and it was recorded. I got off the scale and looked at Doc and used hand gestures.

"What are you doing?"

Doc put his index finger to his lips. No one was aware of what Doc just pulled off except me. I was shocked. He was unbelievable with his pocketbook of tricks. Doc looked at me and winked, and I started laughing uncontrollably. I watched as my opponent stepped on the scale and weighed in at 111 pounds.

Doc seemed to know everybody in the fight game. My opponent was a little older with a stocky build and big forearms.

Doc faced me and started to inform me about the boxer I would be going up against in the ring.

"His name is Al Rollins. He has a deadly right hand so be careful of his right cross."

I understood.

My fight was the sixth bout and we were getting ready back in the dressing room. Doc was taping my hands and putting my new gloves on when the page came in the dressing room and yelled, "Sixth bout, in the ring."

Doc and I went to the ring where Doc lifted the ropes and I entered and sat on my corner stool. My opponent, Al Rollins, was sitting on his corner stool. The referee motioned us to come to the center of the ring and receive his instructions. Doc whispered in the referee's ear that I was deaf and couldn't hear the bell.

"Don't worry, I'll let him know when it's time."

The arena at Saint Anthony's was filled to capacity and I felt the vibrations of anticipation from the spectators. Then the vibration of the bell came through the mat and up through my feet. The fight was on.

Al Rollins' forearms were huge. I tried to feel him out in the first round, but he was bulldozing me. I started using Al Peters' method of watching his gloves rather than looking in his eyes.

He tried a few forearm moves on me, but I was too fast and ducked all his punches. My speed was my asset in this bout. The referee tapped my shoulder to let me know the first round was over. I knew I outscored him in the first round, that I outboxed him.

I sat on the stool as Doc wiped me down with a cool sponge. His lips were moving too fast for me to understand what he was saying, so I just nodded my head and went along like I knew what he said to me. I felt the sweat running down my back. I was loose and raring to go.

The second round bell rung and Doc pushed me into the center of the ring. I stuck my head out a little because I wanted Al to strike my left ear and give me my badge of honor, a cauliflower ear.

Surprised, he threw a left and hit me hard on my right temple. An explosion went off in my head. I was dazed and flicks of glimmering lights were floating around me and then they faded away and my vision started to clear.

Suddenly I heard unfamiliar sounds. The crowd was cheering and yelling came from the back of the arena. Then the bell sounded.

The second round was over. I was trying to cool myself and get control of my senses.

Al Rollins woke up something in me, I heard sounds and my voice was there although I couldn't utter a clear word, only inaudible mumbles.

I went back to my corner and tried hard to make Doc understand that I could hear. My uttered words were garbled, but I could possibly talk. He was trying to prepare me for the third round.

"Keep jabbing, Danny! Keep up the good work!"

I hear the third round bell ring and the crowd whistling and cheering. I get to the center of the ring and jabbing at

Al Rollins to keep him away from my ear. I am so scared he will hit it again and my hearing and voice will go as fast as it came. I feel that my right ear is swollen and that maybe I finally have a cauliflower ear.

The third round bell rings. I go back to my corner while the referee stands in the middle of the ring scratching his head. He comes over to my corner.

"Did you hear the bell?"

"Yes. But I can't believe it."

I mumble and point to Al Rollins' corner as if to say he made it happen when he hit me in the right temple. Doc Reiner's eyes are as big as silver dollars filled with tears that start streaming down his face. He knows he has witnessed a miracle.

The ring announcer comes into the ring to announce the results of the bout and calls us to the center. The suspense of the outcome is taking forever. I am hardly able to contain myself. The ring announcer raises my arm.

"The winner, Danny London."

I shook hands with Al Rollins. I got a brand new fully loaded fourteen-karat gold wristwatch from the announcer. I shook his hand and thanked him.

We go back to the dressing room. I take a hot shower and get dressed. I am still dazed from the result of the fight, not the win but the unbelievable birth of sound.

Doc and I go to Al Rollins' dressing room and I try my best to thank him with words, but I can't utter the correct pronunciation of the sounds so I kiss his head and tightly bear hug him. I suspects he understands.

At this moment in my life I feel reborn and given a second chance at life. My handicap no longer exists and can't hold me back from my big dream. Now it is up to me to take full advantage of what the Lord, the universe, and whatever and whoever is involved in making this miracle happen not be taken for granted. At this moment, I am blessed and I know it.

10

When I get home I am out of my mind with excitement. I rush in and blurt out my news to my family that I can hear and talk. At first, the room is silent with disbelief, and then the room erupts with joyful yelling and phrases of happiness. My family can't wait to hear the incredible story of what just happened in the ring. My vocal cords are rusty from years of no use, and my words are crude and hard to understand, but they are coming out and my family has tears in their eyes knowing I am blessed with a miracle from God.

I was fighting Al Rollins, a more experienced fighter than me and older. He punched me in the right temple and a bonging sound came into my ears. I felt sounds come from my mouth and surrounding sounds woke up my ears and I tried to tell everyone I heard and was able to speak even though the words were not clear. Everyone looked at me amazed.

"I won the three-round fight, Pop, and they gave me a gold wristwatch. I want you to have it to remember what happened on this day, the day my life changed forever."

My father was speechless. Funny, he wasn't able to say a word. He held me tight and kissed me. His happiness overflowed from him to me. I knew he was so proud of me. I felt it.

Mom came over and took my face in her hands.

"Not bad, no cuts, no flat nose, and no cauliflower ear. Gain Schloffin. Get some sleep."

I hugged everyone and tried to say good night. It didn't sound quite right but they knew what I meant. I went to my room to look at my face. No cuts or bruising and no sign of a cauliflower ear.

"To hell with a cauliflower ear!"

I realized I don't want to get hurt and banged up in the ring. Boxing is about laying a glove on the other guy. I don't need any scars or a flat nose or a stupid cauliflower ear for people to know that I'm a boxer. They'll know soon enough who I am.

I left my room and walked softly to my brothers' room and took the radio from the bedside table. I returned to my room, locked the door, plugged in the radio, and turned it on full volume. The sweetest jazz sounds came floating in my ears and I fell asleep to the soothing sounds of music. It was two o'clock in the morning when I woke up to banging from the ceiling and yelling to turn off the radio.

I got out of bed and banged back at them. I was shocked that my family never came in and yelled. Maybe they were sleeping deeply and snoring loudly. I fell back to sleep and when I woke the radio was off, and I suspected that one of my brothers turned it off. I looked again at my face in the mirror and opened my mouth to look at my tongue. I closed it and tried to whistle. I whistled and started making sounds.

Danny London

I ate a hearty breakfast and left the apartment feeling like a new person, I was a new person. I was proud of myself and gained confidence not only with my boxing, but with my ability to speak and hear. Now I was able to communicate and socialize. Lip reading and signing were difficult for me and many times things that were said would be misinterpreted.

As I started to talk to people and friends my words came out wrong and my sentences were awkward and usually backward. People who really didn't know me thought that I didn't speak English. I was frustrated, upset, and discouraged, but I kept on talking and listening to other peoples' words. A month passed and I begun to speak a little better and somewhat clearer with the help of so many friends.

I hadn't heard from Doc Reiner so I went to Pitt Street Gym and ran into him there.

"When will I fight again?"

"Danny, I want you to take a month off from the ring and find a day job so you can train at night. I want you in shape for the Golden Gloves which starts in the winter."

I was really anxious to get back in the ring, but I learned Doc always pointed me in the right direction. A fear started taking over my thoughts. I kept visualizing a blow to the head and the world becoming silent. However, the words from Doc about competing in the Golden Gloves Elimination Contest boosted my spirits and for now the fear faded.

I followed Doc's advice and was hired as a delivery boy earning twelve dollars a week. I still turned my salary over to mom who gave me two dollars a week as allowance. I was never satisfied with this arrangement, but this is the way it was.

My working during the day and training at night kept me out of trouble on the streets. I was in peak shape and ready to fight. I received a postcard from the Golden Gloves Elimination Board to come down to their office for a physical examination. I passed my physical, but they disqualified me, because they found out that I falsified my age on the application. I was only fifteen and you had to be sixteen to enter the Golden Gloves Elimination.

Somebody ratted on me, someone who knew me. I wanted to find the coward and knock him down with a right cross. I was on fire, a mad dog ready to attack and tear the snitch into pieces. Doc and I never found out who informed the board, but in the end it didn't matter, the damage was done. I was disqualified from amateur boxing until I was sixteen years old.

"Doc, what will I do until I'm sixteen?"

"Don't worry, I have a plan. We're going to change your name to Joe Friedman and go to New Jersey to fight."

Doc took me to New Jersey and I got my amateur card there under the bogus name. I was thrilled. I fought three times there and won all three.

That year, 1929, all hell broke loose with the economy and people were going broke and bankrupt. My father lost his cigar store and the bank lost all his money. My father was out of business with no way to earn a living, which was the case with so many other businessmen.

My father became good friends with a man by the name of Mr. Weiner who lived in our apartment building and was a house painter by trade. He asked my father if he wanted a job painting houses. He had plenty of work and needed another hand. Mr. Weiner treated my father well and taught him the house painting business and after a few months my father left him and went into business for himself as a house painter.

He bid on a couple of big jobs and got them. He wanted his sons, including me, to help out in his house painting business. Sammy, Eddie, and I were painting in a customer's house when my father told me to paint a wall. Dad left the room and I was alone. I made a giant mess; paint was all over the beautiful hardwood floor and me. When my father came back in the room to check how I was doing, he went ballistic on me, cursing, yelling, and stomping around. The commotion caused my brothers to come running to see the problem. They were embarrassed by the mess I caused, and stood paralyzed with gaping mouths. My father continued to call me every vulgarity in the book.

I was on fire. I threw the brush down and yelled. My painting career came to a sudden end.

In 1930 my parents decided it was time to move from the dirty slum of Pitt Street to Coney Island. They found a comfortable apartment in a two family house in a beautiful neighborhood on Twenty-second Street.

The entire family helped with packing the furnishings and the move. We couldn't afford a moving company. The cost to carry everything in the apartment down six flights of stairs was too expensive, so we did it all. It was difficult, and the hardest part was getting the old piano out of the apartment, which my parents insisted on taking. My brothers and I decided to lower it with a rope out of the window. I was totally amazed that no one was injured or

John J. Morabito

killed that day. Everything was accomplished, everything fit in the moving truck, and we were off to Coney Island, our new home.

11

Everything fit well in our new home. It looked as if we lived here forever when it was finally all fixed up. I never told Doc Reiner that I was moving and he'd be surprised when he had to walk up six floors looking for me and find no one home.

I took a nice walk on the boardwalk and the ocean air felt refreshing and the seawater aromas were so much better than the old slum smell down on Pitt Street. I was thrilled that my parents made the move and I was part of it all.

The mornings were special for me at our new address. Each day I would get up early and run two miles on the boardwalk. The cool air from the ocean made me feel healthy and invigorated. A few weeks passed and I went to the BMT Coney Island Train Station, because I decided it was time for me to go to Brooklyn. The fare was five cents and it took an hour to get to the east side and it was a slow torturous boring ride for any person to endure.

The old neighborhood looked exactly as I remembered and the people I knew were glad to see me and greeted me warmly. Everyone was curious about what it was like living in Coney Island.

"It's fine, I like living near the boardwalk and the ocean, but the train ride is long and monotonous. I thought I'd never get here."

My sentences were still a bit crude and hard for some people to understand but my hearing was near perfect and I knew in time with a little hard work I'd become better at pronouncing words and speaking.

I went into my old apartment building and walked up the five flights to Mutty's apartment. Benny and Issy, his brothers, were there and glad to see me. His parents hugged and kissed me. Mutty's mom made a delicious meal and we ate and talked and reminisced about the old times.

After my visit with Mutty and his family, Mutty and I left to walk around the neighborhood and we ran into Mr. and Mrs. Weiner, my father's good friends. He told me that they were moving from Pitt Street to Coney Island. I knew my parents would be elated to have their friends close.

"Mutty, I haven't seen Doc Reiner since we moved and I never had a chance to tell him I was moving, so I'm going down to the gym to see if he's around."

"I haven't seen Doc Reiner in a while. He's normally on the corner or in the candy store near the gym."

I thanked Mutty and told him that I would be in touch and headed down to the corner candy store where Doc hung out. It was one of his second homes along with his buddies and if he wasn't there, then he'd normally be at the gym. I waited at the store and then went to the gym. No one had seen him and he was nowhere to be found.

A couple hours passed and it started to get dark. I gave up looking for Doc and went to the train station and took the long gloomy trek back to Coney Island. I thought about Doc the entire ride. Was it my fault he was gone because I hadn't told him about the move? Maybe he thought I gave up on boxing and him? Maybe something happened to him and he was in the hospital and no one knew.

When I got home supper was on the table and the family was altogether, but I wasn't too hungry. My thoughts had drifted back to Doc. I couldn't get him out of my mind. I was disappointed that I couldn't find him.

A week or so had passed and again I went back to Pitt Street and looked for Doc. Again he wasn't there and no one saw him or knew his whereabouts. His disappearance was totally out of character for him. I was confused and concerned.

I continued to work and made pocket money. My morning routine of roadwork was part of my life now. My goal was to stay in the best shape possible and find a way to get back in the ring. I longed to box and was itching to get back in the ring to compete and win titles. Because of Doc's disappearance, I had no direction and guidance. I was on my own.

I was sixteen and my sister Annie knew a man named Mr. Potash, a tap dance instructor. Annie was interested in dance and she took lessons from him. He taught her how to tap dance and she became so good, they became partners in a nightclub and performed a few vaudeville acts together. As time passed Annie mentioned to Mr. Potash that I was an excellent amateur boxer.

Annie came to me and told me that Mr. Potash had a connection with a man who was a big boxing manger and could help get me professional fights.

"Annie, I can't do that. What will Doc Reiner say?"

"Danny, Doc Reiner is nowhere to be found. No one has seen him and he hasn't been in contact with you at all."

"Okay, Annie. I'll take a chance and go with Mr. Potash to see this big manager guy."

I met Mr. Potash and he took me to Forty-ninth Street and Broadway in Manhattan. We took the elevator to the twelfth floor and went to the office door marked BOXING ENTERPRISES in gold leaf letters. We walked right in and Mr. Potash introduced me to a large man with a weird name that I couldn't pronounce. He glared at me intensely, never shook my hand or asked my name. I guessed he was a real big shot.

"How many fights have you had?"

"Fourteen amateur fights, won ten and lost four by decision."

The big gorilla condescendingly looked me up and down. "You don't look big enough or old enough to fight professional bouts."

The big palooka thought he knew me, but he had no idea who I was, and I didn't need him or his put-downs. He just used people. Well, I wasn't going to give him the chance to judge me.

"See you some other time when I'm ready."

I grabbed Mr. Potash's arm. "Let's get out of here."

Mr. Potash agreed that this was not the man for me. We took the train back home to Coney Island.

Annie was waiting for me when I walked in the house.

"How did you make out?"

I told her the whole story and she was frustrated with the outcome of the meeting, but she knew when the time was right, doors would start opening for me and I knew that this was not the time and not the man for me.

12

Mr. and Mrs. Weiner moved from Pitt Street to Coney Island. They and my parents visited each other daily and were enjoying each other's company. Their relationship became stronger as they were always there for each other if anyone of them needed something. It was nice to see my parents socialize after always working so hard all the time.

Mutty started to come by my house in Coney Island more and more. We spent more time together. We took a walk on Surf Avenue and Thirty-first Street and found a poolroom with a gym upstairs. The sign over the door read HALF MOON GYM. Mutty and I went upstairs to the gym and were watching the fighters train and it brought back many old memories for me. I felt homesick. No one knew me or that I was a boxer.

The owner of the gym was Issy Caplin, brother of Hymie Caplin, who was the manager of Al Singer and Ben Jeby, world champion boxers. Many local professional and amateur fighters trained here.

"Mr. Caplin, what does it cost to train here?"

"Three dollars a month."

"Mutty, if I trained here I won't have to travel to Pitt Street and waste so much time. It'll be much easier. I can start training next week."

Issy Caplin just looked at me and didn't ask any questions.

"Okay, see you next week."

I walked out of Half Moon Gym with Mutty whistling. I was happy. I could begin to train again in a great gym. Mutty and I went to the boardwalk where I treated him to a couple of hot dogs, ice cream, and popcorn. After that we jumped on the giant Ferris wheel, biggest in the world. By the time we reached home our stomachs were grumbling and we were nauseous from eating so much junk and going round and round and round. We threw up our guts for an hour.

I found a job at Happy's Lunchoenette on Coney Island. I worked from 8 a.m. to 4 p.m. five days a week and a half day on Saturday. I made twelve dollars a week, which wasn't too bad for the area. My boss was Harry. He liked me a lot and was a nice guy.

I joined the Half Moon Gym and began training at night from six to nine. Issy watched me train for a few nights and finally approached me.

"Who's your manager?"

"Doc Reiner."

"I'm a friend of Doc, I know him well. Is he still your manager?"

"I don't know because I haven't seen him in over two months, I don't know where he is. Do you know where he is?"

"Doc and I go way back. He's been a single independent guy for as long as I've known him. But he has reached an age in his life where his financial security was nil. Now,

I'm with a very select few of Doc Reiner's friends who know of his longtime relationship with a very well-to-do, successful surgeon's wife. She had a special attraction to Doc and recently her husband suddenly passed. Word has it that Doc and the wealthy widow are living in the South of France."

My ears were now put to a test and I couldn't believe what I was hearing. I thought I knew all about Doc, I thought we were solid friends, but maybe there is a secretive side in everyone's life.

"Maybe I should give Doc a little more time, he might show up, but if he doesn't I just might take you up on your offer."

"Danny, Doc is gone and you're not going to see him again. I'm sure he misses you, but that's life and the reality. Did you have a legal binding contract with Doc?"

"No."

"That's good then there's nothing legal binding you to him. I'll wait for you to make a decision."

I spoke to the people at the candy store and at Pitt Street Gym again and gave them my new address to give to Doc if he showed up. Two weeks passed and I never received any communication from Doc. It was time to make a decision on what I needed to do. I wanted to start fighting again.

I thought about Annie who was smart and knowledgeable about negotiations. She could talk to Issy Caplin and explain to me what he offered to do as my manager. She worked days so I waited for her to come home and after dinner I asked her to talk to Issy.

"Sure, Danny, sure. Set up a time and we'll find out what's on his mind and take it from there."

The next night Annie and I went down to the Half Moon Gym and sat with Issy and they talked.

"So, Issy, what's the deal?"

"I would like to train and manage your brother to fight professionally. I can arrange fights that will pay him well and make him a better boxer."

"Danny's only sixteen, how do you propose to get him professional fights when he's required to be eighteen years old?"

"I can make this work. I'll get him a phony birth certificate making him eighteen and have your parents sign the application for the boxing license, then he'll begin his career."

"Sounds good to me. How about you, Danny?"

"Sounds great!"

About a week later we received the documentation and Issy and I went to the Boxing Commission and Issy paid the ten-dollar application fee for the license. I took the receipt home to show my parents and they were happy and proud. A few days later a letter came from the Boxing Commission. I opened the envelope and my new boxing license was there with my picture. I was now legal to fight professionally. I thought this day would never come and it was here, finally.

I went over to the Half Moon Gym and showed my license to Issy.

"I'll come over to your house tomorrow night at eight to talk to your parents and you about signing a three-year contract."

Issy came with his fashionable cigar tucked in the corner of his mouth. He was a short stocky guy who was honest and easy to understand. He met my parents at eight o'clock and he went over the terms of the contract with me in front of my parents. I agreed to the terms and signed it.

"Danny, I have scheduled a fight in Carnarsie in two weeks against Benny Amster. It's a four-round bout and I want you to start training first thing tomorrow at the Half Moon Gym."

"I'll be there."

Benny Amster was my first professional fight. I was in good shape but felt I needed to get stronger. The Half Moon Gym was good for exercising but not for finding sparring partners. I told Issy about this problem and he understood and agreed that he'd find me sparring partners.

The next day Issy took me to Saint Nicolas Gym on Sixty-sixth Street in Manhattan. The gym had three boxing rings, five heavy bags, and four speed bags. The place wasn't well lit, dark and dingy, but there were plenty of sparring partners always ready to spar.

I started training at Saint Nicolas every day and stayed in optimal physical shape. Issy was a seasoned trainer and had a knack for managing. My sparring partners were all professionals and I got what I asked for, well-trained professional boxers who tore me up.

The best boxers trained at Saint Nicolas—Kid Chocolate, Al Brown, Black Bill, Mickey Walker, Phil Tobia, Joey La Grey, and even Jack Renault. They were all the great ones and I sparred with them. I was keeping the best company in the boxing world and I became their friend.

The fight night arrived and I had to go through the formality of weighing in with the Boxing Commission. My opponent, Benny Amster, got on the scale before me and weighed in at 115 pounds. I stepped on the scale and weighed in at 113 pounds. I felt good about my weight. I was ready to fight.

Issy took me home and told me to eat and get some rest. My mother cooked me a juicy porterhouse steak and a baked potato loaded with butter. I took a nap for a couple of hours and then got up to get ready. About six thirty Issy picked me up and we drove over to Carnarsie Arena. We went right into the dressing room when we arrived and Issy taped up my hands.

The first bout of the evening ended in a knockout and they carried that boxer out of the ring on a stretcher. They entered the dressing room and laid him on a table near me. He never moved a muscle. He was knocked out cold. I looked at his still body with only his chest moving up and down slightly, and the jitters started to take over my body. What's my fate, I asked myself.

A boy came in the dressing room and yelled, "Fourth bout, fourth bout in the ring."

I took one more glance at the fallen guy and beads of sweat started building on my forehead. I jumped to my feet and started throwing jabs to loosen up and Issy led me out of the dressing room toward the ring.

From the corner of my eye I saw my brothers and sisters standing in the stands yelling and cheering my name. I waved and smiled and my confidence blossomed. I went to my corner and looked across the ring and looking back at me was Benny Amster. The announcer entered the center of the ring.

"In this corner, hailing from Coney Island, New York, is Danny London."

The cheers and whistles from the fans got my blood above my knees.

"In this corner, from the Lower East Side of Manhattan, Benny Amster."

The cheers were thunderous.

The bell rang and I came out and circled Amster. I quickly landed two solid jabs and then he got me in a clinch. I looked in the stands and saw Annie, her lips mouthing, "Come on, Danny! Come on, Danny, give it to him."

I stepped back, looked straight at her, and winked. The crowd went into an uproar of laughter. They loved it and me.

My strategy and early training from Doc paid off. I flashed on Doc and heard jab, jab, my core training. I outboxed Amster in all four rounds.

The ring announcer and the referee motioned us to the middle of the ring.

"Winner by unanimous decision, Danny London."

I shook hands with Benny Amster and on the way back to the dressing room I smiled to myself, I was glad I was not the guy on the stretcher. Issy met me outside the dressing room.

"You boxed like a true champion, Danny."

My family tried to enter the dressing room but they were stopped by the police at the entrance and had to wait outside. As I came out they all jumped on me and showered me with kisses, handshakes, and pats on the back. I felt great, everybody was happy and I was a winner in my first professional fight.

We hung around until the main event was over and Issy received the purse money. He gave me forty dollars and didn't take a cut. He said that the win was all mine until the purses got bigger.

My brothers and sisters and I went home to Coney Island, and the ride home was filled with continuous laughter, praises, and love. My mother and father waited up for me and when I walked in they looked me over from head to toe. My mom looked me over a second time.

"No marks on your face Danny. You won your first professional fight."

"That's right, Mom, all the bruises are inside my brain."

Everyone broke out laughing including me and then my dad walked to my side and put his arm on my shoulder.

"David, you keep punching. Don't let anybody hit you."

My mother piped in with her favorite Jewish phrase. "No Mach Gelt? Mach Gelt?"

"Sure, Mom, money."

I pulled the forty dollars out of my pocket and handed it to her. I watched as her eyes doubled in size and her jaw dropped. She kissed me and started rambling in Jewish. I didn't understand a word she said and neither did anyone else. Suddenly exhaustion overtook me. I kissed everyone and went to my room for some much needed sleep.

I slept soundly all night, and when I went downstairs in the morning a big breakfast was waiting for me. After breakfast, Mom handed me ten dollars for pocket money. I went out to the local candy store and bought a newspaper and turned to the final fight results.

DANNY LONDON OUTCLASSES BENNY AMSTER IN FOUR ROUNDS

There weren't any details on the fight, but I didn't care. It was my first pro fight and I won. People in the neighborhood greeted me with compliments and handshakes of congratulations. I felt high as a kite, soaring above the clouds. I took a long walk on the boardwalk and returned home.

13

The economic Depression of those times hit many people hard. The biggest hit was lack of work, no jobs. People tried to get relief from the National Recovery Administration (NRA) and President Franklin D. Roosevelt created the Civilian Conservation Corps (CCC), putting thousands of unemployed Americans back to work on projects with environmental benefits.

The Depression also took its toll on boxers. The Boxing Commission reduced the amount of money per round to five dollars for all local boxers. For the main event, the winner received a percent of a one hundred-dollar purse.

Almost every week the Boxing Commission called me to substitute in emergency bouts, where a boxer couldn't make the fight.

Things changed for me when Issy came to me and explained that he had to sell the Half Moon Gym for financial reasons. The good news was that he was still going to be my manager, and he was appointed the matchmaker for Saint Nicolas Arena. He assured me that he would always try to get me a fight and keep me on the substitute list for emergency bouts. Issy had a connection with Madison

Square Garden, so he also placed me on their emergency list as well.

I waited in the dressing room at Madison Square Garden for my match.

"Emergency bout next."

I wasn't scheduled to fight until the fourth bout, but someone was knocked out and the next fighter hadn't showed up yet. So they said that I was next. I hadn't changed into my boxing gear, I still had my street pants on, my hands were not taped and my boxing shoes were on the floor. I rushed around and dressed and a trainer quickly put my gloves on. He laced up my boxing shoes and we headed for the ring.

I got to the ring and looked in my opponent's corner. There was Lou Farber, a highly touted fighter with an impeccable record.

I held my own with Farber. He was smart and fast and I boxed him like a real professional. I knew in the end he respected me even though I lost the fight in a decision. I won one hundred dollars. Forty went to Issy Caplin and the rest was mine. Things were tough at home and I knew Mom would be happy with the money. When I got home I gave her the sixty dollars and she gave me ten. I told her I lost by a decision and she kissed my cheek.

"Better luck next time."

I kept fighting for almost three years. I had fifty fights under my belt. I fought two and three times a week but the money never seemed to be enough. Issy took his cut that left me with next to nothing. My parents were getting frustrated with me. I argued with them about my boxing. They didn't understand. Continually they called me names and cursed at me.

When the money was short, they were not so supportive. They wanted me to fight more and bring more money into the household. I wondered where the happiness and pride they felt went after my first professional fight. I figured it disappeared with the money. I became angry and discouraged with them. But I calmed myself down thinking of what my parents were going through raising a family the size of ours. I needed to help out just as the rest of the family was doing.

My brother, Willie, who was a merchant marine, had a family of his own and he was in trouble. I got word that he was in jail for not paying alimony and child support. I went to visit him at the county jail and he was extremely happy to see me.

"Danny, you're the only one from the family who came to visit me. Thanks, brother."

"That's a shame. I'm sure they know you're here."

He stared at me with a blank look on his face, frozen. He was speechless. Then it hit me. Willie was away at sea when I regained my speech and hearing. I sat down and told him my story and when I finished he was crying uncontrollably. After he regained his composure, he just kept shaking his head and thanking God. Finally, we were able to continue our conversation with an intermittent, "Thank you, God" from Willie.

"I'll be getting out next week and I'm leaving for Los Angeles to find work."

"I'd like to go with you, maybe I'll get some fights out of town and make money."

"What about Mom and Dad? What'll they think?"

"Things are not good at home between us. They call me names and put me down, I think we need a break from each other. They need money and I can't get any significant paying fights. It's difficult for everyone."

"You're welcome to come along with me when I get out, see you next week."

"I'll be outside waiting for you, brother."

I kept busy for the next week. There was no Half Moon Gym to train in and no fights scheduled, so my days consisted of roadwork on the boardwalk and trying to stay in shape. After a two-mile run on the boardwalk, I went home and on the front porch was a man standing wearing a suit. I was in a heavy sweat, hot and tired.

"Are you Danny London?"

"Yes, I'm Danny London."

The man extended his hand. "My name is Robert Ripley, owner of *Ripley's Believe it or Not*. I want to interview you about the miraculous occurrence of regaining your speech and hearing after so many years. I heard you were punched in the right temple by Al Rollin during a boxing bout when the miracle occurred."

We sat on the front porch for more than an hour, I told him about the event in detail and how this experience changed my life.

He was awed by the unbelievable outcome of a single punch. He asked my permission to put my story in his book, *Ripley's Believe it or Not*. I thanked him for taking the time to come and see me, and that I was honored to be part of his book.

14

I woke up early the next day because Willie was getting released from jail. I put some personal items in my small leather gym bag with my gloves, shoes, and trunks. I packed my heavy flannel shirt, hat, and leather jacket. I headed down to the county jail to meet Willie. The day was clear and when the large iron door swung open, Willie walked out. He stood there for a moment and took a deep breath of fresh, free air before he came over to me. He grabbed me and hugged me tightly.

"Danny, are you ready to leave?"

"Sure, I'm ready. What'd you think I'm here for?"

"Do you have a change of clothes and your toothbrush?"

"Everything I need is in this bag, Mr. Funny Man, and if it's not in here then I don't need it."

Willie had ten dollars and I had twenty dollars. We put our money together and agreed that we'd share everything.

"Danny, we need to go to New Jersey to catch a freight train west. We'll have to wait for night, so the yard bosses won't catch us. They can be pretty mean with their night sticks."

Willie knew all about the train routes and he had a map in his head on which trains went where and how to get on the right freight train. Willie was a real hobo. Willie told me that he was taught to jump trains by the king of hobos, Jeff Smith, who was his best friend.

It was getting dark and Willie pointed to a train that was moving about ten miles an hour.

"There's our train, follow me."

We ran alongside of the freight train and got real close to it. Willie grabbed onto the ladder and lifted himself into the open boxcar. He looked out at me and I did the same thing and landed in the boxcar. Within minutes, the train was speeding up to fifty or sixty miles an hour. The boxcar's floor was covered with large pieces of paper that we used to make our beds. We slept soundly all night as the freight train headed west.

In the early morning we felt the freight train slowing to about fifteen miles an hour and we knew that it was time to jump off before it reached the yard. The yard bosses were there ready to enforce the rules to violators, and we were violators. We jumped off and headed to the highway where a sign read, "Cleveland 3 Miles."

We walked for a while and came to a truck stop. I thought it was fate because we were hungry and cold. We entered the diner and went directly into the men's room and washed our faces and hands. We sat down at the counter and ordered bacon, eggs, pancakes, and coffee. We were stuffed by the time we left.

We went into Cleveland and walked around Main Street for most of the day, then headed down to the freight yard. We waited for night so we could catch the next freight train west. Willie found a brakeman and found out the next train was due to leave for Chicago at 9 p.m. from Track 12.

The brakeman was a nice guy and helped us. He warned Willie that the yard boss was a mean son of a b——h, and we needed to watch our backs because he had no compassion for hobos. Willie thanked him and since we had plenty of time to kill we went to the grocery store and bought some supplies. We bought a loaf of bread, can of beans, a large pound cake, and a half gallon of milk. We returned to the freight yard at eight o'clock and waited patiently till the train pulled in exactly at nine o'clock.

The train was stopped and waiting for Willie and I and the passengers to get on. Willie opened the door halfway and we climbed in. There was no paper so we just lay out on the wooden floor and the train started creeping slowly away. It rose to a speed of sixty miles an hour within a few minutes.

The clacking of the wheels on the train was irritating and aggravating but the more I rode the more I got used to the noise. It became soothing, a sedative that lulled me to sleep. I was so glad I packed my heavy jacket and wool cap. The nights in the freight cars were chilly and without a cover. It was cold especially because of the high speeds of the train.

A few hours passed and Willie nudged me to wake up. "Are you hungry?"

"I'm more hungry than I am tired."

Willie took out his knife and opened the can of beans and made a couple of sandwiches, one for him and one for me. We followed up with a piece of cake and some milk.

"Danny, do you want some more to eat or drink?"

I was full so Willie put the rest of the food away. My stomach was content and my ears and mind fell into the rhythm of the big iron wheels clacking on the tracks. I fell off into a deep sleep. The next thing I felt was Willie nudging me again.

"Come on, Danny, wake up. Chicago calls."

It was about six o'clock in the morning and chilly. The freight train slowed to about ten miles an hour and Willie pushed the big door about a quarter of the way open. He had to be very wary of the bulls. The yardmen in the big cities were tough and knew how to wield their nightsticks against desperate men known as hobos.

We jumped out of the boxcar and walked to the highway. We walked along the highway quite awhile before we entered the city of Chicago. Chicago was similar to New York City. It was big and busy; full of people, cars, trucks, busses, trains, stores, eateries, and roadside merchandise vendors. We found a restaurant and went to the men's room and washed then sat down and devoured a hearty breakfast.

We left the restaurant, and when we got outside Willie held my arm and told me to keep quiet and follow his lead. We walked to Michigan Avenue and I followed Willie into a tall building. We went to the directory and stopped as Willie studied the information. Then we took the elevator to the sixth floor. We exited and went directly to a door marked JEWISH FEDERATION. We entered the office and a small man approached.

"May I help you, gentlemen?"

I had no idea what Willie was up to, but I did as he asked. I kept quiet and observed.

"We're Jewish and we came from Los Angeles. We're trying to get back home to New York, and I was hoping you could help us with a meal and a place to sleep for the night."

What a lie, I thought, but I did as I was told and never uttered a sound.

"Who is the boy?"

"He's my little brother. He's deaf and mute."

Pitifully the man glanced over at me.

"Follow me."

We followed him into a tiny office and he went directly to his desk. He took two tickets from a top drawer and handed them to Willie. The tickets were for meals and a place to wash and sleep for the night.

"Willie, how did you know about this organization?"

"I've traveled all my life and learned how to survive on the road. If I didn't learn how to get around we would be up s——'s creek without a paddle."

It was early in the day, so Willie suggested we find the local gym and watch the fighters train. We found a drug store and went inside to the phone booth and looked up the address of a local gym in the yellow pages.

We found the gym and walked upstairs. We watched the fighters train all afternoon. To my surprise, two of the greats were right in front of me—Barney Ross was sparring and King Levinsky was working out on the speed bag. I waved to them when they were finished and they winked. Great boxers crossed my life in the past and presently two were right in front of me.

"Let's go and have some supper."

We had a fine meal using our meal tickets and then we went over to the Jewish Center and checked into our room.

The room smelled fresh with clean linens and had a shower with plenty of hot water and soap.

We washed and quickly retired. We peacefully slept all night, our bodies grateful for the comfort and silence. Oddly, I didn't miss the clacking of the iron wheels on the train tracks.

The morning came too quickly. When I opened my eyes, Willie was standing over me saying that it was time to get up. We got our stuff together, went to a diner, and ate an awesome breakfast. We were rested and content when we left the diner. We headed for a grocery store where we purchased some supplies for the next leg of the trip. We bought ham, cheese, a loaf of bread, and a half gallon of milk.

When we arrived at the freight yard Willie found the brakeman and inquired about the next freight going south. He found out the next freight train would leave from track 8 at noon. The brakeman emphasized that we needed to be on the lookout for the bulls because they would be out in droves today. We knew to take heed his warning.

"Thanks, we'll watch our step."

We stayed out of sight until the freight train started to move out at a snail's pace. Willie and I made our move to the boxcar. The door was opened halfway. Willie threw our food in first and then we ran and jumped in. When I settled in and looked up, I saw three hobos huddled together, and there were two hobos at the far end of the boxcar looking mean and desperate. They were wide eyed, praying that we weren't the bulls.

They soon realized we were like them, hobos hitching a ride. They nodded hello in unison. Willie and I nodded back. We moved to a corner as the train started to increase speed. Willie struck up conversations with the hobos about freight train hopping techniques and ways of accessing train schedules and destinations. One hobo remarked on his long resume.

"It took me many years and many beatings from the bulls to learn the schedules of the freights and the bulls."

I assumed that now he was a graduate of hobo school.

Willie continued to talk and I became mesmerized by the droning of the conversation and the iron wheels of the freight train clacking on the tracks. I began nodding off to sleep.

Two mean-looking hobos at the far end of the boxcar began mumbling to each other. Their low chatter kept me from falling asleep. They jumped to their feet and made the way over to Willie and me. They were filthy and their clothes were equally grimy. The bigger of the two had stubbles of a beard and between the stubbles were traces of dirt. The second man was wiry with a villainous grin that showed his black and brown decaying teeth. The smaller of the two spoke first.

"Go on, Lester, ask him."

"That's what I'm about to do Grady."

He stared coldly at Willie.

"What you got in that sack, buddy?"

"Some supplies and food that we carried on with us."

"Well, me and Grady ain't eaten in two days."

"Well, I'll make you a sandwich that you can share."

Grady and Lester roared with laughter that smothered the sound of the clacking freight train wheels. Their hideous laughs caught the attention of all the hobos in the boxcar.

"We'll take the whole sack of food and maybe I'll give you a sandwich to share with the boney kid next to you."

Willie slowly got to his feet and I followed his lead. The guys were nasty looking bullies who had no respect for anybody.

I saw Grady reach into his pocket and pull out a jack knife and began to unfold it. Before Willie could respond, I pushed him aside and hit Lester with a strong jab right between his eyes and watched him fold to the floor. Grady waved his knife in the air threatening us. I got my balance and hit him in the mouth with a right cross. Blood splattered all over the boxcar floor along with his decaying teeth. He fell in the middle of the mess.

Three other men rose to their feet and cheered. I felt like I was back in the ring and won a two-round bout. The three men picked up the two thugs one by one and tossed them out onto the side of the tracks. Willie looked at me wide-eyed. Finally he got to see me fight.

"Damn, Danny, great punching power! You'll be the world champ some day."

The excitement was over and everyone went back to their spots and fell off to sleep.

It was late afternoon when I awoke to the monotonous clacking of the wheels. It was endless. The door of the boxcar was opened just enough and I was able to see the bright blue sky and the air felt a bit warmer. I was hungry.

I opened the bag and took out the ham and cheese. I looked around at the other men in the car. They looked like starving poor souls. I called them over and we shared our food. It was a beggars' banquet. They ate like it was their last meal. They were thankful and we were all satisfied.

The locomotive kept pulling fast all day. Through the partially opened door the blue sky began to fade and the night slowly drifted into the boxcar. As the train's pace slowed we knew it was our destination. One by one we jumped out of the boxcar and each went one way or another.

As our routine, Willie and I headed to the highway and there found a signpost, "Shreveport, Louisiana 5 Miles." We made it to a roadside diner and ordered hamburgers, fried potatoes, slices of apple pie, and coffee. The completely satisfying meal cost seventy-five cents. I followed Willie through the city and as always he appeared to know his way around. We stopped at a freight yard at the southern end of Shreveport. Willie relayed our next plan of action.

"At midnight the train will pull through but it won't stop, it'll only slow down to about fifteen miles an hour. We have to run fast to catch it."

"Where's it going?"

"Houston, Texas."

Willie was right on the money. The moon was full and straight up in the sky, it was midnight and the freight was coming through. We took off running hard along the tracks. When we were close we jumped and grabbed hold of the ladder and pulled ourselves into the boxcar. The moon's light shown through the half opened door illuminating the bodies of ten hobos already in the boxcar.

Willie and I found a spot and sat with our backs against the wall. The other men looked like they had been in the boxcar for hours. Their faces showed desperation and hunger and from the smell that wafted in the air they badly needed hot baths. Their eyes were sunken and sad and they had puzzled expressions on their faces. They hoped they would find work somewhere in the next city to change their fate.

The freight sped all night long and Willie and I slept all night long. One of the men kicked Willie's foot to wake him and to let him know that the train was nearing the freight yard. We had to jump off soon.

The sun was just coming over the horizon and the morning air was humid. We jumped off the boxcar and quickly made our way to the long straight highway. We walked for about a mile and came to a road sign, "Houston 3 Miles."

15

It was about seven o'clock in the morning and Willie announced that we were dead broke. We used all our money on supplies. Then, with a broad grin, Willie winked as if to say that it would be all right.

"I'd never let my little brother down."

We walked for about forty-five minutes to a neighborhood in Houston. It still confused me that Willie knew so many places in the cities. We stopped at a well-maintained building, a Jewish synagogue. He told me to sit on the bench across from the temple and wait for him and then he disappeared through the entry doors.

I sat on the bench bored and hungry. I longed to box again. I missed the ring and excitement. I wondered if I would ever be given the chance again. I began to feel like one of the hobos in the boxcar—desperate, trapped, worried about where life was taking me and if I had any control over it.

I thought about my family back home in New York. My mother's image was vivid in my mind. I was overwhelmed with remorse. I was sure she was worried along with the rest of the family. I never said a word to anyone, just left and my actions reminded me of how I felt when I hadn't a clue where Doc Reiner was, as he just vanished from sight. I made a big mistake.

Willie came out of the temple walking with a short man wearing a yarmulke on his head. He introduced him to me. He was Rabbi Goldstein, head of the synagogue. Willie must've told him that I was deaf and mute because he looked at me with sorrowful eyes while he spoke to Willie.

"I want you boys to have a safe trip back to New York."

He reached into a black leather purse and gave me two dollars and Willie two dollars.

"I took a collection from our members and this is the best I could do with such short notice."

My eyes opened up twice their size and I felt so much better that we were not penniless. We thanked the rabbi and told him to thank all the members for their generous donation. We shook hands and left.

"Willie, you got some racket. You know the places to go and the people to see for money and shelter."

"I don't want you to worry. We'll be fine."

We walked to a local joint and ate Texas chicken fried steaks with eggs and hot cups of coffee for twenty-five cents each. My mood rose with the fullness of my belly, I was ready to continue our journey.

We walked and found the local Salvation Army and they gave us a cot to sleep on and a daily meal. We made this our home for the next couple of days. The next morning Willie woke up early and rested.

"Danny, let's find a gym where maybe we can get you a fight and make us some money."

Willie looked in the phone book and found a gym in downtown Houston. It was typical of most gyms, sweaty and smelly, and these aromas were home to my nostrils. The gym was small with little equipment to train. There were a handful of boxers training and sparring, but they didn't look so hot and no one was training them.

"Are you in good enough shape to fight?"

"If we can get a fight, I'll train for a week and get in shape."

I had my bag with my gloves and equipment with me.

"Danny, see that fat guy sitting over there with the big cigar in his mouth? It looks like he's running the show here."

"Yeah, he's the man we should talk to."

Willie and I walked over to the man and Willie introduced himself to him through the blanket of smoke.

"Do you manage fighters?"

"Why?"

"My brother, Danny London, is a fighter and we wanted to know if you could arrange a couple of fights."

"How many fights has he had?"

"About fifty."

The guy stood up and took a long hard look at me.

"I'll try him out. Go ahead in the dressing room and get ready to box."

"Sure."

"I'll get an opponent."

Willie and I went into the dressing room and Willie helped me put on my gloves. He did a fairly decent job of taping my hands. The locker room attendant put a head guard on me and we left the dressing room and headed for the ring. Willie lifted the ropes for me and I stood in my corner trying to get loose, dancing in place and shadow boxing.

I looked to the other corner where a black guy entered the ring. He was stocky and heavier than me. Without a warning, cigar man yelled, "Time!"

The guy charged at me and started slugging wildly. I bobbed and weaved out of his way. He couldn't put a glove on me. In the middle of the second round it was over, the fighter was panting for air and could hardly lift his gloves anymore. We went back to our corners and the fat man approached me.

"You got class and style. Someone trained you well in the art of boxing. I'll manage you but you must sign a one-year contract with me."

My mind flashed back, I had a contract with Issy for three years. What would be the legal ramifications with the boxing commission and Issy if they found out I signed another contract?

Willie told the guy we'd think it over and get back to him.

"Sure, I understand, take your time. I'm here every day."

He reached into his pocket and pulled out a big wad of money and peeled one ten-dollar bill off the top and handed it to Willie.

"Willie, let's go eat. Dancing around the ring made me hungry. I don't need a one-year contract. The guy was nice enough but I have a manager already."

We went back to the Salvation Army after our meal and slept for ten hours. The next day was hot and humid, over ninety degrees. We walked around the city all day and all I thought about was home and my boxing career or what was left of it. Was it turning into a boxcar career? I was sure I was missed at home and in the ring.

The next morning I sat across from Willie during breakfast but I couldn't focus.

"What's wrong?"

"I'm going back home. I'm sure Mom and the family are worried about me."

"Danny, it's up to you, you're the boss of you. If that's what you want, I understand. I'm going on to Los Angeles to ship out as quartermaster on a ship to Europe. Will you be all right getting back to New York alone?"

"You taught me the tricks of the trade, how to get the freight train schedules, hop a train, where to get a hot meal and places to sleep, at the Jewish Federation and Salvation Army. They are holding my reservations. Soon I may be crowned a King of the Hobos."

We laughed until we cried. Willie pulled me close to him and gave me a warm hug, squeezing my head to his.

That evening we stopped at the grocery store and bought some food for my trip back east. I bought a can of sardines, a loaf of bread, a box of cookies, and a half gallon of milk. We headed down to the freight yard and waited about an hour before the train pulled in.

Willie talked nonstop about how I regained my ability to speak and hear. He remembered every detail of the event just the way I told him. He was so emotional and at the end we were sobbing.

"Danny, you're a true warrior. I know in my heart with all you've been through in your young life only great things wait for you in the future. I am so proud to be your brother. Can't wait to see your name in lights. Danny London, Champion of the World."

It was midnight, and the train slowed down as it came into the yard. I ran and threw my food and bag into the boxcar. I jumped on the ladder and climbed inside. I stood in the doorway as I waved good-bye to Willie.

"You'll be the next champ someday."

As I was the only one in the boxcar, I sat in a corner, folded my arms, and thought. My brother is a good guy. He has a big heart and is full of love. I'll miss him. The clacking of the wheels on the tracks did its job and I was sound asleep by time the freight train reached a clicking-clacking sixty miles an hour.

I woke early in the morning and ate. I felt the train slowing. I hopped off and made it to the next location to catch the next train east. While traveling back home I did everything that Willie taught me. It all worked out fine, I never ran into a problem. I had a lot of time to think. I thought about myself mostly and my desires in life, and decided when I got home I'd be a new man. I wanted to start over and do things right this time.

16

The freight train slowed as I got on my feet, looked out and saw a familiar sight New Jersey. I was right back where Willie and I started. It took me two weeks to get back home, after traveling more than two months.

I finally got back to New York, a city I was able to maneuver around with ease. I was way up town on Forty-second Street when my stomach started talking to me. I had seventy-five cents left and went into Chock Full of Nuts Coffee Shop. I ordered two large donuts and a cup of coffee that left me with enough money for a train to Coney Island.

I felt good as I left the coffee shop and started walking down Forty-second Street heading for the subway. A young man down on his luck stopped me.

"Spare change, sir, spare change."

I felt for him. I knew the look of desperation, the pathetic stance of hitting rock bottom. I traveled with men that looked exactly like this young man. I had experienced having no money and no place to sleep or eat. I had a dime to spare and handed it to him. I told him that it was all I had. He thanked me with a warm handshake.

"God bless you."

I stood in the subway station waiting for the train and felt secure encircled by the familiar surroundings. I wondered how my family was going to react when they saw me. It would remain a mystery until I walked in the house. I boarded the subway and headed to the last seat in the car. I was dirty and my clothes were ragged. I didn't want anyone to recognize me.

I got off the subway at Coney Island and walked down Surf Avenue. On the corner of Twenty-first Street at Aaron Bing Chevrolet dealership, my brother Jack was on a stepladder painting the side of the building. He saw me going into the local candy store and practically fell off the ladder leaning to get a clear view. When he was positive it was me he jumped off the ladder and ran to the store. Out of breath, he stumbled in and began hugging and kissing me and then started rambling.

"Danny, what on Earth are you doing here? Where have you been? When did you get back? We were so worried. You crazy fool."

So many questions at one time I didn't know which one to answer first.

I felt exhausted and hungry, but I had to tell Jack the entire story of my journey with Willie, everything. Jack was awed and told me I was lucky to be alive because Willie was a crazy son of a b——h. I couldn't stop laughing because I knew he was right, Willie *was* a crazy son of a b——h.

"You better get home. Everyone is so worried and concerned about you, especially Mom and Dad."

I gave Jack a hug and walked slowly down Surf Avenue. I feared walking into the house not knowing the reception I'd receive. When I finally arrived and walked in, no one was home. I went into my bedroom, undressed, and threw my clothes in the garbage. I filled the tub with hot water, got in, and soaked, feeling safe and comfortable. I was so relaxed I almost fell asleep. By the time I got out of the tub, I was a squeaky clean wrinkled prune. I put on my bathrobe and went to my room to relax.

When I opened the door my mother greeted me with a bear hug and a million kisses all over my face.

"Why did you run away from home?"

"Mom, please don't ask me any questions."

For once she listened and changed the subject.

"How are you feeling?"

"I'm fine, just tired and weary from a long trip."

My mother handed me two newspapers.

"You should read these stories about you."

I looked at the newspaper and started to read the first article.

> Danny London, local fighter, missing for over a month, disappeared from the area.

The second article was just as horrifying.

> An all-point bulletin and a missing person's report was filed for local boxer, Danny London, who disappeared from the area over a month ago. Anyone with information please contact the local precinct.

"Great publicity, but you better inform the police that I'm alive and well and home."

"Danny, you always helped support our family and we needed you here. I'm so afraid you might desert us again."

"Mom, I'm staying. I will train again and fight to make money to help support and take care of you. I'm sorry I left."

She embraced me and held me tight for a long time. I finally had to pry myself from her grip of steel.

"I'm so tired, Mom. I'm going to sleep now. I'll see you for breakfast."

As soon as my head hit the pillow I was asleep. In the comfort of my bed, I felt safe and slept soundly all night.

I woke early the next morning, jumped out of bed, and opened the curtains. It was a beautiful morning, sun shining in a bright blue sky. I got in the prone position and did twenty push-ups, then went downstairs to the kitchen in my bathrobe. Everyone was there including my dad.

"Hello, everyone."

The family broke out into laughter and I excused myself and said that I would be right back. I ran upstairs, put on a pair of slacks, clean shirt, and polished shoes. I returned to the kitchen.

"Sorry I kept everyone waiting."

Annie stood up and looked directly into my eyes.

"That's all right, we've been waiting for over two months for you."

The entire family was in stitches. The roar of laughter never ended as each sibling hugged and kissed me and welcomed me home. My mother made a huge, hearty breakfast and we talked and ate without any friction.

"Mom, the food is delicious, there's no place like home."

She came over and kissed me again and again and again and again until I finally collapsed.

I looked at my brothers and asked them if they wanted to take a walk on the boardwalk. We went for a long, slow-paced walk and I told them how our brother, Willie, took me on an adventure halfway across the country. I talked about the freight trains and hobos; the Jewish Federation, the Salvation Army, the manager in Houston, and my long journey back home all alone. They listened intently. They said that it was the most amazing story they ever heard. It was hard for them to believe that I did all that. I thought they were a little envious of their little brother.

When we returned home, they were still asking questions. They were concerned about Willie, but I assured them Willie was capable of taking care of himself. Mom had a lunch fit for a king waiting for us. I felt closer to my brothers after our long walk. They listened to my story and asked questions. They cared about my life and my dream.

Lunch was scrumptious and the conversation continued. When lunch was over I told my Mother that I was going to see my friends and would be back for supper. I took the train to my old neighborhood and found Mutty. He was so happy to see me, another barrage of bear hugs.

"Where did you go? When did you get back?"

"I went away with Willie."

Mutty listened to my story and was wowed by my encounters and experiences.

"I figured you weren't getting along with your family, but I never thought you would vanish like you did. I felt my friend abandoned me, so please don't do that again. I'm so glad you're back."

Mutty was really like a brother to me. He always stuck up for me and explained things to me that I couldn't understand. I was wrong to leave him with no explanation. He deserved more.

"Have you seen your manager, Issy Caplin? Does he know that you're back home?"

"I haven't seen him yet, but after I rest for a week or so I'll go see him and explain how I felt about fighting for five dollars a round, that has to change."

"Yeah, you're a professional now and things have to get better for you. You worked hard to train and fight and you are worth more money."

"What have you been doing?"

"I've got a pretty good job with a captain of a fishing boat down at the bay. We go out all night long and fish the Long Island Sound. We sell the catch at the fish market. The pay is okay but the hours stink."

Mutty was an honest guy and he never got himself wrapped up with street politics or associated with hoodlums. He held allegiance to his friends and family.

"Mutty, so glad to see you. Come by and see me when you can and I'll stay in touch."

I left Mutty and felt our relationship and friendship were as strong as ever.

I took the slow boring train back to Coney Island and arrived home around five o'clock to the smell of mouth-watering food from the dining table where the family sat waiting for me and my father to come home.

My dad came in right behind me and sat down beside me at the dinner table.

"How are you doing, David?"

"Fine, Dad. I'm feeling fine."

We ate a tasty roast chicken with mashed potatoes and devoured an entire chocolate cake baked by Annie. We paired the slice of cake with a hot cup of coffee and it hit the spot. Dad started the conversation.

"Danny, did you go see Issy Caplin yet?"

"No, I'll rest for another week and then go see him and explain everything."

"Good, because you're still under contract and he should know what you're planning."

"You're right, Pop. I'll start roadwork next week to stay in shape, then I'll go see Issy."

17

For the next two weeks, I did what I promised myself to do. I woke each morning and did roadwork to stay in shape. The healthy diet I kept stopped me from eating crap sold on the boardwalk. My mother's cooking helped me eat the right foods with high nutrition.

After my roadwork I went to the train station and took the subway to Manhattan. It was time to see my manager, Issy Caplin. I went to the building where his office was located and I took the elevator to the fourth floor. The new Danny London wasn't nervous at all. He was confident in what he wanted to accomplish. I would tell Issy the truth about where I was and what I did and I couldn't predict his reaction.

I walked in his office and he was sitting and at his desk typing. He looked up and glared at me and then he pressed down hard on his cigar.

"A fine partner you are. Where the f——k have you been?"

"Take it easy, Issy. I was disgusted with my family and had to get away for a while. Are you going to blame me?"

"You should've let me know. I'm your manager. I was worried and concerned about you. No one knew where the hell you were."

"It was a spur of the moment decision and I didn't tell anybody what I was doing."

"How long have you been back?"

"About two weeks."

"You should've called me when you got home."

"I needed to rest and get back in shape and that's what I did. I'm in terrific shape and ready to pick up where we left off."

"Are you ready to train with me and get back in the ring?"

"Yeah, I'm ready. When and where?"

"We'll train at Stillman's Gym. Be there tomorrow morning."

"Well, it's about time. I always wanted to train there."

Issy reached into his pocket and took out a ten-dollar bill and handed it to me.

"Here's a little spending money, but please behave and let me know what's on your mind from now on."

I went home feeling happy. I told my family about my meeting with Issy and that I was training at Stillman's Gym starting tomorrow morning. They were not satisfied with the way Issy managed me. They believed he could do much more. I explained that I had to follow his lead until this contract ended. The contract would not last forever and if I ever got a new manager I'd never sign a contract again.

The conversation ended peacefully and everyone including my father agreed with what I had to do. They respected my decision and they knew I couldn't sign a contract with anyone else or go anywhere until I was a free agent.

Danny London

I woke early the next morning, stretched, washed, and ate a light breakfast. I put my boxing gear in my gym bag and headed for the front door.

My mother kissed me good-bye.

"Good luck to you."

I took the train to Manhattan and hurried to the gym where Issy was waiting for me.

"Danny, I want you to meet your new trainers."

He introduced me to Whitey Bimstein and Ray Arcel who were known in the boxing world as the best in the fight game. I couldn't believe I moved into the big league. Issy Caplin came through. He paid for my gym expenses and set me up with the best. He had my back. I went to the locker room and dressed in my workout gear.

"Where do you want me, Whitey?"

"Go upstairs and start working out on the floor. Do three rounds on the heavy bag, two rounds on the speed bag, two rounds shadow boxing, two rounds skipping rope, then end with a half an hour of floor exercises on the mat."

I had a great first day working out at Stillman's. It was exciting to see prestigious boxers there. It was exactly what I needed, surrounded by the greats to watch their techniques and training habits and learn.

The train ride back to Coney Island wasn't boring this time. I went over my workout routine in my head and I felt like a new man with a new life.

I walked in the house and sat down at the dinner table with the rest of the family. In between bites of the porterhouse steak and baked potato and sips from my tea, I told my family about the greats in the gym and the two infamous trainers who were my trainers. They were amused by my childlike excitement. I was working with two of the top-notch trainers in the business. I was on top of the world.

After I trained hard for two months, I started traveling to New York, Brooklyn, New Jersey, Long Island, and Massachusetts to compete in bouts. The intense schedule of fights became tiring. The frustration of not making enough money continually ate at me. It was a tough time in the country and it was difficult to get the main bouts because there were too many hungry boxers trying to fight for the top money. I went back to Coney Island to take a break from the hectic fight schedule and get some needed rest.

Mutty came over to my house to visit me with a new friend, Al Tesh, a big husky guy from Russia. When I shook hands with him, his big hand covered mine completely. Al became a good friend to me. He kept me company and we saw each other and hung out just about every day.

One day Al and I were walking down Twenty-Seventh Street and Mermaid Avenue and we stopped in the poolroom on the corner, where two brothers, Murry and Hymie Miller, were the proprietors. They were tough guys that didn't take any s——t from wise guys who attempted to start trouble in their place. If any jerk started any trouble, Murry and Hymie would be gentle but firm and escort them out.

Hymie walked up to me and heartily shook my hand and said that he was a big fan.

"Danny, when will you fight again?"

"I'm taking a rest for a few days, but I'll be back soon."

From that day on we all became friends. Hymie and Murry showed a great deal of interest in my boxing career.

"Danny, if you ever need a manager I would like to be that guy."

"I don't know, Hymie. Maybe someday we can work something out."

A couple days later, Al Tesh and I were playing a game of rotation in the poolroom. After Al beat me, I went over to pay for the time and Hymie refused to take my money.

"Your money is no good around here, Danny. You and your friend Al can play as much as you want and it's on the house."

"Thanks, Hymie."

The next day Al and I were back in the poolroom playing a game of straight pool. My mother passed by and saw me through the window. She turned back and started yelling and cursing at me through the glass. A guy from the poolroom tells me there's a woman out there calling for me.

I turned around and my mother was standing at the poolroom door.

"You dirty bum, playing pool. Why aren't you at the gym training to fight so you can make some money for me? You can't make any money playing pool."

Her craziness had to end. As I glanced around the room all the guys were staring at me. I was so embarrassed and humiliated by my mother's crazy tirade of profanities. She was acting like a nut. I was infuriated. I walked outside and she came running after me.

"Mom, stop! Take it easy!"

I shouted and startled her so that she stopped yelling and looked at me.

"What are you worried about? I need to take a rest. Don't you think I get hurt when I fight?"

I was perspiring so badly, the sweat was running off my forehead like a waterfall. I was so mad I couldn't even speak anymore. I stood in front of her huffing and puffing. My mother turned and walked away cursing.

Hymie came to my side and put his arm around my shoulder.

"Danny, let it go. Mothers can't relate to the lives of boxers. She has no idea what it takes to be you."

"Thanks, Hymie. I need some fresh air."

Al and I went for a walk on the boardwalk and talked about boxing and before I knew it I was home. Al said that he would see me soon and left.

I walked into the house and confronted my mother.

"What's wrong with you treating me like a baby in front of my friends, making a fool of me? I can't take your craziness anymore."

"I'm sorry I didn't mean it."

"You say that all the time, but you always forget and do it all over again."

My father was in the other room and heard us arguing. He came in the kitchen and I told him about Mom's meltdown in front of the pool hall.

"From now on, stay out of Danny's business. He can take care of himself. He's a young man, not your baby. Leave him alone, do you understand?"

His words were loud and clear and he was trying desperately to control his temper.

My mother served dinner as my father continued to holler at her. I thought maybe now she realizes how horrible her behavior made me feel and she feels belittled like she made me feel.

After supper I waited until things calmed down and went over to my mom and hugged her tightly. I loved my mother and I knew she loved me. She was just wound tight and always worried about money that at times, like today, drove her over the edge.

There was a knock at the door and Jack yelled that it was for me. It was a telegram. I gave the delivery boy fifty cents and I opened the telegram.

> You are scheduled to fight six rounds against Patsy LaRocco at Ridgewood Grove Arena this Saturday night. START TRAINING! See you tomorrow.
>
> Regards
> Issy Caplin

Ten minutes later Al Tesh knocked on the door. He came in and I introduced him to the family. I told him about Saturday's fight and he said that he would like to go with me. I told him he was welcome.

18

The next day I went to Stillman's Gym and met with Whitey Bimstein. He was an excellent trainer and knowledgeable about the importance of a boxer being in the best shape possible before a bout. He orchestrated an extremely hard workout program for me that morning. I sparred with some of the best boxers in the city.

Whitey did his homework. He investigated my opponent, Patsy La Rocco, and let me know his strengths and weaknesses so I would be prepared in the ring. Whitey was a no-nonsense trainer. He trained me in both the physical and psychological parts of the boxing game. His partner, Ray Arcel, reinforced everything that Whitey did. They were a great team and I was glad to be on it. I was totally ready for Saturday night's fight.

Two days before the fight I went to the poolroom to see Hymie to let him know that I would be fighting Saturday night at Ridgewood Grove.

"I know all about it, Danny. I read about it in the newspaper. I'll be there to cheer you on. I'd never miss it."

"Thanks, I'll see you at the fight."

I sat in the dressing room while Ray taped my hands and Whitey went over last-minute instructions for me. He emphasized that Patsy La Rocco would come out punching and continue banging on me, nonstop. We entered the ring and I scanned over the spectators and found Hymie Miller. He gave me a good luck wink and I winked one back at him.

The ring announcer started his introductions and when he announced Danny London from Coney Island, all my fans stood and the arena erupted with their whistles and applause. I was motioned to the center of the ring by the referee for last-minute instructions when I got a close-up look at Patsy La Rocco. He was mean looking, serious face, big arms, and a strong body. Whitey told me that he was an excellent body puncher and could inflict real harm.

The first round bell rang and before I even reached the center of the ring, La Rocco was on me like a bulldozer. He plowed right into me and began to rough me up. I had to jab and stiff-arm him for the entire six rounds. I outjabbed him every round and he couldn't keep up with my fast-paced footwork. I kept away from his deadly body punches because he was so heavy on his feet. I knew I was winning by points.

After the sixth round bell rung, we went to our corners. I fought a damned good fight and was sure I had the win in the bag. The ring announcer came to the center of the ring with the judge's tallies and announced the fight a draw. I was shocked. I couldn't believe it. I walked over to La Rocco's corner and shook his hand.

"Good fight."

As I walked to the dressing room, the crowd booed and threw garbage into the ring at the announcer. Their uproar continued for a long time. The referee quickly left the ring and ran out of the arena. Once in the dressing room, I was greeted by Whitey.

"You got robbed, Danny."

When Hymie and Al opened the door to the dressing room, I heard the crowd still yelling their disgruntled remarks as they left the arena. Hymie walked straight to me.

"Danny, you fought a beautiful fight. You were the winner in my eyes."

Al stood and shook his head in disbelief.

My hometown fans and friends waited outside the arena and when I left they cheered and patted me on the back. They were telling me that I was their winner.

The next blow I received was outside the ring. The guaranteed sixty-dollar purse for the bout turned out to be thirty-five dollars, another letdown. The upside was no marks on my face and no cauliflower ear.

My brother, Jack, and a couple of his friends were at the fight, so we loaded into his 1930 Ford and drove back home to Coney Island. The family was waiting up for me. My mom made coffee and we had coffee and cake. I began to feel better. As usual, my mother inspected my face.

"Thank the good Lord you don't have any marks on your face."

I gave her twenty-five dollars and she gave me a million-dollar grin and showered me with kisses all over my mark-free face.

We talked and joked around until three in the morning and finally, totally exhausted, I fell into bed.

19

It was 1932 and I turned eighteen years old. The summer was extremely hot and the humidity was outrageously high for days on end. The gym was stifling. The high heat made training unbearable and boxing became a battle. The more water I drank, twice as much poured out of me. I struggled to fight in the hot weather.

I was at the Fort Hamilton Arena fighting Tony Morengo when in the sixth round the temperature reached one hundred degrees. Both Tony and I were sluggish using every ounce of energy we had left just to finish. The crowd booed that they were not happy with us and that they wanted to see a fight. They didn't care about the heat and they showed us no mercy. Our arms felt heavy as granite. We were doing the best we could do, but we were exhausted from the sweltering heat.

The sixth round bell sounded and it was music to my ears. I won by decision. I was completely drained. I was lifeless. I didn't care about the win. I was too hot to care. I went back to the dressing room and spoke to Izzy.

"I can't train and fight in this hot weather. The heat's killing my body and spirit."

"Fine, give me a call when you're ready to start again."

Jack took Al and me back home. The temperature never broke and I invited Al to stay over. We rolled and tumbled in our beds and sweated our butts off until I couldn't take any more.

"Let's go sleep on the beach, maybe it's cooler."

We took our blankets and a couple of bottles of water and walked down to the beach. We went near the water and laid the blankets out. It was cooler and the sound of the waves put us to sleep within minutes. When the sun came up the heat began again and the temperature rose. We gathered our things and went back to the house.

I wanted to rest during the hot summer. I couldn't train in the extreme heat. Most of the time, I'd go down to the beach by myself and lie down under the cool boardwalk. Some people liked to sunbathe, but that was not for me.

One time while passing time under the boardwalk, I smelled smoke. I jumped up on top of the boardwalk and I looked in the direction of the giant billboard advertising a motorcycle daredevil show. Behind the billboard I saw bellowing smoke and flames coming from the direction of Surf Avenue. I ran over and realized the fire was on my street. The steady wind from the ocean fueled the fire and it intensified igniting one house after another including mine.

Panicked, I ran through the firemen, who tried to stop me, yelling that my baby sister Marilyn was in there. I bolted to the entrance engulfed in flames in my bare feet and bathing suit when I was jolted backward and thrown to the ground. A fireman standing over me said that he was in the house and checked every room and the house was vacant. Relieved, I put my head in my hands and mumbled, "Thanks."

The entire block was on fire and most of the houses were burnt to the ground. The firemen fought the fire for hours, but it was impossible to control the overwhelming flames. When the fires finally burned out, only charred skeletons of homes remained. The devastation of the fire rocked the entire community.

People walked around in circles. They cried and moaned searching for their families and neighbors. Still in my bathing suit I began searching for my family. Walking down Mermaid Avenue in a daze, I ran into my neighbor, Mrs. Cane, who was sobbing.

"Mrs. Cane, do you know where's my family?"

"They're at the Knights of Pythias Lodge on Twenty-First Street."

I hugged Mrs. Cane and started running to the lodge because I needed to see that my family was safe. My feet were burning on the hot pavement. When I entered the hall I ran into a wall of people; I had a hard time maneuvering through to find my family.

Finally, I spied Annie waving to me. I ran over and she was crying. Annie was so upset because there was no insurance on the house. We had nothing left.

"We have no clothes, no shelter, and no money. We have nothing, how will we survive?"

Annie answered through her tears. "The Red Cross and the Salvation Army will supply everyone with clothes and shoes."

And Annie was right. The next day, the Red Cross and Salvation Army gave us clothes and shoes. I received a shirt, a pair of pants, and shoes that didn't fit. They were too big and I gave them back and told them that someone else might be this size.

I went to Mutty's and he gave me some of his clothes and shoes until I was able to buy new ones of my own.

My dad had no money and we had no place to live. So my dad and I went to see my father's brother, Uncle Eddie, who lived on Ocean Parkway in Brooklyn. He was wealthy, making his money in real estate. My dad explained his situation and he borrowed a few hundred dollars from Eddie with the understanding he'd pay it back when he got on his feet.

A few days passed, and my family with many other families moved to a Red Cross shelter. I was invited to stay at Mutty's until things got better. Jack worked as a mechanic for Aaron Bing at his Chevrolet dealership on Coney Island. Aaron Bing heard about the tragedy and gave my parents one hundred dollars to help them out. He was a generous man with a good heart. I told Aaron Bing that when I made enough money fighting I would pay him back. He was touched.

"Don't you worry, it's my pleasure to help."

My father found an apartment in a three-family house near the bay. He bought living room furniture, beds for the bedrooms, and a kitchen table and kitchenware for Mom. He bought new clothes for himself, Mom, and us. No one in the family knew how much money he spent on the new furnishings and clothes. Every month he paid installments on his purchases.

We started to be a normal family again, dinners every night together and a clean place to lay our heads. It was comforting to be together again.

20

Jack was doing well at Aaron Bing Chevrolet as a mechanic and he became good friends with Aaron Bing, the owner. Aaron asked Jack to tell me that he was interested in me and wanted to manage my boxing career. Jack told me that Aaron wanted to meet with me and discuss the boxing business.

"Danny, Aaron Bing is wealthy and he'll give you anything you want and take good care of you."

"Tell Aaron I'll think it over and get back to him."

I thought hard about the deal that Aaron offered and decided to go and talk to Al and get his feelings on it all.

"It sounds like a sweet deal and Aaron has the money to take care of your career. What about your existing contract with Issy Caplin?"

"I have about four months left on my contract with Issy, and then I'm done. I haven't been too satisfied with Issy's handling of my fights. He's not a bad guy, but he always seems to skim on the purse money with me."

"It's up to you. If you're not happy with Issy then you should set up a meeting with Aaron and listen to what he has to offer."

I had Jack schedule a meeting with Aaron and I asked Al to come along and listen to the conversation. Al and I entered the building and graciously Aaron greeted us and led us into his private office. We sat down and Aaron began to talk about how he would help me advance in the boxing world. I felt that he was honestly and sincerely interested in my well being.

"Danny, I'm not completely savvy in the world of boxing, but if I manage you, I'll learn. I'll make it a priority to get you more fights and bigger purses. I promise I'll take care of you and you won't be sorry that you gave me a chance. I'll draw up a one-year contract and put in a stipulation, if at any time you're unhappy with how I'm handling your career, the contract becomes null and void on your command."

I looked at Al and I knew he was thinking what I was thinking. I still was under contract with Issy Caplin.

"Well, it sounds like a great deal and I want you to manage me, but I'm under contract with Issy Caplin for four more months before my three-year contract expires."

"Okay, how about I give Issy a call and see what he says about you getting out of his contract and changing managers."

"Sure, why not? Give him a call and see what he says."

Aaron found Issy's phone number and called. "Hello, Mr. Caplin? My name is Aaron Bing and I'm sitting here with Danny London. Danny's interested in signing a boxing contract with me as his new manager."

"Danny London is under contract with me."

"I know, and according to Danny the contract expires in four months."

"Danny signed the option of the contract that stated he'll be under contract with me for three more years."

"Mr. Caplin, it's obvious that there's a miscommunication between you and your client. I'll discuss the mysterious signing of the option with Danny."

Aaron hung up and went over the details of the conversation with us.

"Another three years with Issy, oh no. He tricked me down in Atlantic City at the Lenox Arena. I remember, just before my fight with Mike Belloise, a four-round bout that I lost, my trainer asked me to sign the contract. I'm a stupid ass. I didn't read it and I didn't know what I signed. I feel so dumb."

"You really didn't know what you signed and they never explained it to you?"

"No, they didn't. If I knew I wouldn't sign it."

Aaron prepared a letter to Issy Caplin stating that I was ignorant about the contract because it was never explained or discussed with me, so therefore it was not legal. I was given the contract by the trainer to sign and Issy was not present and this was also illegal. The letters between Aaron and Issy went back and forth for days. Issy was irate and threatened that he was taking the issue to the Boxing Commission.

A few days later, I received a letter from Commissioner William Muldoon of the Boxing Commission. He scheduled a hearing at the Boxing Commission Office in Manhattan. I went to the hearing with my father and Aaron Bing. We sat at a long table across from William Muldoon, Bert Strand, and other members of the commission. Issy Caplin sat at the far end of the table with his face all poked out. He was pissed off.

Aaron Bing had his ducks in a row. He presented valid documentation that made William Muldoon and the board members understand what happened with the optional contract.

"Mr. London, are you absolutely sure you want Mr. Aaron Bing to be your new manager?"

"Yes, I'm sure, Mr. Muldoon."

"Then I rule, the extended three-year contract was not signed legally and Danny London's contract with Mr. Caplin is over."

My father walked to the end of the table and offered Issy Caplin his hand. He was sorry that my relationship with Issy had to end this way. Issy stood up and shook my father's hand.

"Good luck, Danny. No hard feelings. I wish you great success and hope you're the champ someday."

Issy Caplin walked away with his head held high. This was the name of the game and he did what he had to and so did I. I was glad there were no hard feelings on either side. Aaron Bing was my manager and I was elated and relieved. We shook hands and Aaron took my father and me to a fabulous restaurant to celebrate our new partnership. We ate big, fat juicy steaks and drank a fine bottle of wine. We toasted to a successful partnership for all. After dinner, Aaron drove us home in his new Cadillac, I really could get used to this luxury.

When my dad and I walked in the house the entire family and Al were anxiously waiting to hear the results of the hearing. The second the door closed behind us Jack shouted, "What happened?"

In unison we shouted back, "We won!"

The family erupted with cheers. Al came over and picked me up and squeezed me. Everyone in the family felt that I'd have a brighter future with Aaron Bing as my manager.

The next day Al and I went down to meet with Aaron at his office. Aaron was as excited as I about our future together. I signed a one-year contract and we shook hands. He gave me one hundred dollars to buy boxing equipment to replace what I lost in the fire.

Al and I went up to the Everlast Boxing Factory, the same one I went to with Doc Reiner. After, we went directly to Stillman's Gym. Previously, Aaron spoke with Whitey Bimstein and Ray Arcel and they agreed to continue to train me.

They worked me hard, harder than when I was with Issy. They were the best trainers I could possibly have. They knew all the best methods to prepare a boxer for a fight. They screamed and hollered at me during the workouts, they pushed me to the limits. They would accept nothing but my best effort.

I was driven to become the best fighter I could be. The support from my trainers was music to my ears. They told me that one day I'd be the champ. Their words gave me the incentive to train harder and smarter.

Aaron Bing set up a meeting with a matchmaker, so after the training session, Whitey Bimstein and I went. The matchmaker set up a fight with Joe Tagg's manager. Joe Tagg had just come off his seventeenth straight knockout. He was on a roll and I was anxious to fight him.

I informed Al about the meeting with the matchmaker, and he and Aaron called Joe Tagg's manager and set up the fight. It was scheduled for September fifteenth at the Coney Island Arena. I felt right away that the location gave me a slight edge fighting on my home turf. Al told me that if I won the fight Aaron had a surprise for me, a new car.

I'd try my best to win the fight, a new car plus a substantial payday for the win. Maybe now things would come around in my favor.

September fifteenth was just a week away and I was in the best shape of my life. My body was strong and fit. I developed muscles I never knew I had, my mind was clear of worries, and my mental attitude was positive. The week flew by. I thought about all my past fights, my wins and my losses. This was not just another fight, this was one for my record. I was a top-ranked professional and this fight meant more than any of my other bouts.

Finally Friday night arrived and we entered the arena. Every seat was occupied and every piece of floor space was taken. The crowd's mumbling sounded like a million bees buzzing around their hive. I entered the dressing room where Whitey Bimstein was waiting.

"Danny, I have a detail about Joe Tagg that we unfortunately missed during training. He's a south paw."

I was flushed and confused. I didn't prepare to fight a southpaw. I had to use a different fight strategy with a southpaw. I was a ten to one underdog and the bookies were having a field day. Geez, what about the car?

"Holy s——t, I should've known that crucial piece of info from day one of the negotiations."

Clearly, Whitey and Ray were embarrassed and mortified. They had no answer. While taping my hands, they gave me pertinent information and instructions about techniques used to fight a southpaw. Barely looking at me, they put on my gloves and we left the dressing room. The crowd went wild when I entered the ring and when Joe Tagg entered the ring the crowd yelled even louder. The roars were electrifying and the entire arena was on fire.

The intense stomping and cheers made it feel like we were fighting for the featherweight championship of the world. The crowd knew Tagg's record, and they and the press, sitting ringside, were waiting for his eighteenth victim.

The ring announcer went through his formalities as did the referee, and Joe Tagg and I shook hands and went back to our corners. When the first round bell rang, Tagg came running across the ring wildly throwing haymaker punches. He never touched me. His right hand jabbed the air like an engine's piston and his so-called deadly left continued to miss me. The bell rang and the first round was over. I went back to my corner and sat while Whitey wiped my face down with a cool sponge. I was surprised that he didn't give me any instructions.

The second round was the same as the first. Joe Tagg continued his strategy. He was determined to hit me with a knockout punch and end the fight. I watched him and focused on his gloves. He was telegraphing his punches by intensely watching my moves. The bell rang and the second round was over and he still couldn't put a glove on me.

The third round bell rang and I went to center of the ring and circled Tagg. My timing was perfect. I threw a left hook and a right cross and he went down. The referee gave a ten count and the crowd took the roof off the arena. The press box was quiet. Everyone had their heads down writing, and they couldn't believe what just happened. I ran back to my corner and looked at Whitey and Ray.

"Did I tag Tagg out?"

They erupted into laughter.

I broke Joe Tagg's record. The crowd continued to cheer and chant my name. Al and Aaron jumped in the ring and came to my corner. They inspected me, just like my mother, to make sure I wasn't injured. They jumped around and hugged each other like two kids who just won a baseball game. Al picked me up, put me on his shoulders, and carried me back to the dressing room.

So many fans and friends followed us to the dressing room and tried to get in but the police blocked the door. They removed my gloves and I went into the shower. I wasn't thinking about my win against Joe Tagg, my thoughts were on the new car. I didn't want to say anything to Aaron because I didn't want to ruin his surprise. After my shower, I got dressed.

The win money was dispersed and Aaron ended up with seventy-five dollars. He said that it was my cut after the trainers were paid. There still was no mention from Aaron about the car.

When I left the dressing room, my many deaf and mute friends greeted me. They shook my hand and signed congratulations. I was so happy to see them. So many friends and neighbors patted my shoulder.

"Great fight, Danny. Keep up the good work."

Jack and Al ushered me to the car, and Jack drove us home. It was a cheerful ride with both of them going over the fight blow by blow. As usual, when I entered the house my mother was waiting to look me over to make sure there were no marks and no cauliflower ear. She kissed me and congratulated me. There were about twenty-five people at the house celebrating my first knock out fight. My mother made coffee and served cake to all.

We had a memorable time and everyone left about three o'clock in the morning. I went to bed tired and happy, but I still wondered about the car.

21

I awoke the next morning at eight thinking about the fight, it was my fifty-eighth professional fight and I won by a knockout. At eighteen I fought a highly touted fighter. I dressed in a sport shirt and a new pair of slacks. I went downstairs where a delicious breakfast waited for me prepared by my mom. I handed her fifty dollars and she thanked me.

While I was eating breakfast, I thought about the new car. I wanted a car, and now it was all I thought about. I thought Aaron would probably give me a sports car because of the great win. For now I just had to wait for my surprise from Aaron to arrive. Al finally showed up at my house around eleven o'clock.

"Danny, how do you feel this morning?"

"I'm feeling fine. I'm waiting for Aaron to say something about the car."

"Aaron wants to see you today."

"Let's go and meet him."

In my mind I thought great, he has my car. We walked to his showroom and went into his office. Aaron was dressed in his usual attire, a three-piece suit with a dashing colorful tie. He was clean-shaven and every hair on his head was in place. When he finished his call, he hung up and came over to me and shook my hand.

"You fought a great fight last night. Tagg didn't land too many punches."

"He's got a hard punch and I took a couple of them, then I had to Tagg him out."

Heartily they laughed at my joke. When Aaron regained his composure he handed me one hundred dollars.

"What's this for?"

"It's a small gift for knocking Tagg out."

I was confused and upset. My stomach was doing summersaults. He mentioned nothing about the car. When Al told me about the car, he made it sound like a sure thing, a promise. Now it appeared Aaron was going back on his word.

"Danny, take it easy for a while until I line up more fights for you."

"Okay, Mr. Bing."

Al and I left the showroom. I was surprised, disappointed, and insulted by Aaron for not giving me the car as he promised according to Al.

We walked down the boardwalk and it was time for me to confront Al, so I opened my mouth and cleared the air.

"Why didn't he give me a car?"

"I didn't know he promised to give you a car."

"What are you talking about? You told me that if I won the fight against Joe Tagg he was rewarding me with a car. Either he lied or you lied, which is it?"

"Maybe he gave you a hundred dollars instead of a car, maybe he was just kidding. This is my fault. I should have kept my big lousy mouth shut."

I exploded. "That's it! I ain't takin' no s——t from anybody no more. I'm sick of people taking advantage of me. I guess it'll never change."

We never said another word on our walk home.

I knew Al felt bad, but I didn't care. He was right and he should have kept his big mouth shut. I gave my mother fifty dollars and I told her that Aaron Bing gave me a gift for the win.

"Why are you so upset and sad?"

"Mom, please don't ask me any questions right now, I'm just tired."

Al went home and I went to my bedroom and threw myself across the bed. Again, I was thinking of leaving, I didn't know what to do. I felt betrayed by my friend.

Two weeks passed and I was still mad. I didn't want to see Aaron again. Al went to see Aaron and Aaron shared his concern.

"What happened to Danny? Why hasn't he come to see me?"

"I told Danny that you were going to give him a car if he beat Joe Tagg."

Aaron started laughing uncontrollably. He said that he was joking. "I gave him a hundred dollars for beating Joe Tagg. You never should have told Danny if you weren't sure. Now you endangered our relationship. Straighten it out!"

Al came over and explained that the car thing was a misunderstanding. I didn't care that he said that he was joking. I was pissed off and it changed the way I felt about Aaron and I couldn't let it go. I decided to go and see him.

Al and I walked into his office and I let him know that I didn't think it was right for him to make a joke from a promise. It came down to me believing his word meant something. I told him that he could no longer be my manager, he tarnished our relationship and I no longer trusted him. I was sorry and I wanted the contract back. He gave me the three-month-old contract. I thanked him, shook his hand, and said that I hoped we could remain friends. I walked out into the fresh air and tore the contract into pieces.

I continued to hang around Coney Island, where I did some light roadwork up and down the boardwalk. My attitude was soured. I felt I was right back where I started—nowhere. My disillusionment with boxing and people was an opened sore that festered.

A month later I went to see Mutty. I told him the whole story and that I was fed up and leaving for California. Mutty and I talked about our lives for hours, and then he grinned and looked me straight in the face.

"I'll go with you."

I went home that evening and told my mom and dad that I was leaving for California. I needed a change. My mom was upset, but I explained that I couldn't get any fights here and the fights in California paid more. My mother was still against me going and she pleaded with me to stay and wait it out here. My father was also concerned about me leaving, but he tried to be supportive.

"Do you think it's any different in California?"

"I don't know for sure, but I'm going to find out."

"If you have your head set on it then go and see if the fight game offers you more out there. You'll never know if you don't try."

Finally, mother resigned herself to the fact that I was going.

"Do you need any money?"

"No, I have some money."

My father gave his last bit of advice. "David, please make the right decisions when you get there. Be careful and don't sign any contracts."

He smiled and winked and I went to bed.

22

The next morning, I woke up feeling enthusiastic about leaving and finding a future for my career out west. I kissed everyone good-bye and tried not to let the tears of my mother affect me too much. The rest of the family wished me good luck and safe trip.

It was early in November and the temperature was cooling down. The Atlantic was calm, and I thought that soon I'd see another ocean on the other side of the country. I walked out the front door and was greeted by Mutty sitting on the front porch. He was full of life.

"Are you all set to go?"

"Let's go west, young man."

I explained to Mutty our travel arrangements and he was all excited over the adventurous plans. Our first stop was New Jersey where we would wait to catch the freight train at midnight.

"How do you know what train to catch and where it'll end up?"

"Willie taught me all the tricks of the freight train business, and if we need more help we'll talk to the brakemen. But we have to keep a diligent eye out for the bulls, these yard men carry night sticks and they'll beat the crap out of anyone they catch jumping on the trains."

Mutty and I had some time, so we went to the grocery store and got some food to hold us over until we reached our first stop.

The train pulled in at midnight, right on time. We jumped easily into the boxcar and were facing six hobos huddled in the car lying against the wall. It was a cool night and the train pulled along at sixty miles an hour. We found a spot near a corner to lie down and no one bothered us. The clacking of the wheels put us both to sleep. I awoke to one of the hobos opening the boxcar door about a quarter of the way to let some needed fresh air in. The sun was up and the train was slowing to a stop. I asked him if he knew where we were.

"Lima, Ohio."

The train slowed to about ten miles an hour and it was time for us to get off before the train entered the freight yard. The hobos jumped off the train and Mutty and me followed right behind them.

Out of nowhere the yard bulls came from every direction yelling for everyone to stop. They carried shotguns and nightsticks and they surrounded us. They shoved us along to a cabin in the freight yard.

Some of the hobos looked pretty bad, they were worn out and hungry. One bull stood out as the leader ordering everyone around with a harsh deep voice.

"Line up and face the wall, you good-for-nothing bums."

They searched everyone and confiscated money and anything else of value. When they reached Mutty and me, they made us take off our shoes. The lousy bull found forty dollars in my shoe and thirty dollars in Mutty's shoe.

Every man lost something. We couldn't do anything. We were at their mercy. They had weapons and we knew they'd use them. One hobo had a look of hate on his face, I knew that he wanted to kill the bastards, but knew he'd be the one dead if he tried anything. Another hobo pleaded with a bull to leave him a dollar to get some food, but he pushed him to the ground and kicked him hard. Then I heard the bellowing scream of the head bull.

"Ten minutes to get your ass off the property and get out of town. If we catch you again you'll spent six months in jail and I'll visit you daily, you f——g low lives!"

We rushed out of the cabin without a cent to our names and as we ran, we heard the bulls laughing and joking about their pockets lined with our money.

Lima, Ohio, was an average size city. Mutty and I needed to eat and find a place to sleep before we caught the next train west. I tried to think like Willie and asked a man if he knew where the Salvation Army was located. He gave us directions and we found it. We were given a hot meal and a cot to sleep on for the night. After a night of much needed sleep, we were given a light breakfast along with the many other down and out residents. We were thankful for the accommodations and food.

Mutty was totally out of his comfort zone. Brooklyn was his home. We were broke in a strange city and we didn't know a soul. I had to get us out of this predicament and think fast on my feet. We needed to make a quick buck. I checked a phone book and found there were no gyms and no pool halls in Lima, Ohio. It was a farming town and we weren't farmers.

We walked the streets of Lima and vowed we never come back to this hick town again. It was late when we entered the freight train yard. We met one hobo who pointed us to the right track where a train heading west to Chicago would be coming through at midnight. I met lots of hobos in my life and I came to realize most are decent people who were just down on their luck.

We hopped the freight but slept restlessly all night. We couldn't get the yard boss's harsh voice and the brutality of the bull that inflicted pain on the hobo asking for a stinking dollar out of our minds. We feared meeting up with the yard bulls again. Maybe they were waiting for us at the next stop in Chicago.

The weather was cool and we were tired and hungry. Trying to sleep when you're hungry doesn't work. When we felt the train slow to about fifteen miles an hour we safely jumped out of the boxcar. The sun came up fast while we walked about three miles into the city of Chicago.

We went directly to the Jewish Federation, a place I was familiar with because Willie brought me here. They gave us a hot meal and a place to sleep. The rabbi didn't offer us any money like they did when I was with Willie, but we were grateful for the food and lodging.

The next day we walked around Chicago and then hung around the Chicago Depot. The night came on quickly. We found the schedule for the next train going west, but it was a passenger train. In darkness we made our way to the coal car behind the locomotive where we climbed the ladder each finding a couple of rungs to hold. It was a tough ride. All night long we held tightly to the ladder trying to stay awake and not fall off between the cars. Our fingers were numb from the brisk cool night, the sixty plus miles an hour of the train and the death grip we had on the rung so we wouldn't fall to our deaths.

Finally, it was nearly dawn and the train slowed down just enough for us to jump off. We made it safely to Omaha, Nebraska. We stood on the ground and got a good look at each other. Our hands, faces, and clothes were completely covered in black soot from the coal dust blowing on us all night long.

We walked along the highway until we came to a gas station, where we went into the men's room and washed ourselves. When we left the men's room it was filthy. The sink, walls, and floor were black as coal.

Now we really were destitute hobos looking for a meal. We walked to the center of Omaha and finally found the Salvation Army. They fed us a hearty meal and let us wash in their showers. We felt fairly human again. We decided Omaha was not the place for us. The entire state was one huge cornfield. The city wasn't appealing and we decided not to waste any time here and quickly went to the freight yard.

Night came and we found out from the brakeman that a freight train was leaving at midnight for Salt Lake City, Utah. We felt much better lying on the floor of the boxcar instead of hanging off the ladder of a coal car. This was luxury. The big iron wheels clacked mile after mile heading further west, I was the furthest west I'd ever been. Hunger overcame our tiredness and we were in need of a hearty hot meal.

We never kept track of time. It was either day or night, but our stomachs always told us when it was time to eat. We felt the train slow and I opened the boxcar door. The sun was peaking over the horizon. Mutty and I jumped off the train and made our way into Salt Lake City. Mutty was the designated spokesman on the trip. He had no problem talking to strangers and quickly got us directions to the Salvation Army, which was now our daily routine.

We ate a delicious meal and they gave us a clean cot to sleep on. It was a well-maintained Salvation Army. I asked Mutty to inquire about a gym in the city. The guy in charge was accommodating when Muttty explained that I was a boxer looking for a bout to make some money.

The directions to the gym were clear and we had no trouble finding it. It was located in the heart of the city. We walked in the gym and found the owner, Kid Davis, a former boxer from Salt Lake City. We introduced ourselves and then Mutty did all the talking. He explained I was a boxer from New York and wanted to fight here in Salt Lake City.

"How many fights have you had?"

"Fifty-eight fights."

"Put on the gloves and box a couple of rounds."

I wasn't in great shape but if we were going to make money, I had to show him what I could do in the ring.

"Sure, no problem."

I removed my shirt and left my dirty pants and shoes on. Kid Davis instructed one of his locker room guys to put a pair of gloves on me and he did without taping my hands. I jumped in the ring and saw a well-built black guy in the opposite corner. He was bobbing and weaving, dancing in place and throwing air punches. I weighed about 125 pounds and this guy looked like 130 pounds of pure muscle.

I stood in my corner and stretched a bit and did about thirty seconds of shadow boxing, then Kid Davis yelled, "Time!"

My opponent put both hands up and exposed his midsection. He charged me and wildly threw punches everywhere acting like a crazy man. I knew at that moment he didn't know too much about boxing, so I just began to outbox him. I didn't want to hurt him, so I just let him continue to flail away, never putting a glove on me. In the middle of the second round, Kid Davis yelled, "Time!"

He was taking the gloves off me when the black guy came over.

"Damn, you're hard to hit."

I thanked him for the compliment and shook his hand. Kid Davis finally spoke.

"Danny London, you're a smart classy boxer who was trained well. Are you under contract with a manager?"

"No."

"I can put you in my boxing show next Monday night and in the meantime you can train here, no charge."

We thanked Kid Davis for the opportunity and returned to the Salvation Army. Mutty went and told the manager about the upcoming fight and asked if it would be okay if we stayed there.

"Don't worry about a thing. You can stay here as long as you want."

We were stunned by the kind treatment from this guy.

"Thanks a lot. We'll get you a couple of ringside tickets for the fight."

I trained in Kid Davis's gym for six days straight and felt in pretty good shape. I sparred with Joey Ray, a seasoned boxer in my weight class who trained in the gym. I took Monday morning off from the gym and just did some light roadwork.

Mutty went to the gym and came back to the Salvation Army with no information on the boxer other than his name. I was scheduled to fight a featherweight, Max Mellen. This would be a real test for me in the ring.

Mutty was my lowboy helping me get ready for the fight. He taped my hands and put on my gloves. He found a fairly new pair of boxing shoes and trunks. I was ready for the bout. We headed to the ring and I noticed it was a full house. I thought it was because the locals heard that I was fighting a local boy, Max Mellen. To my surprise, the ring announcer introduced the referee for the fight, none other than the famous Jack Dempsey. This was one of the best moments in my life. I was awed by the great heavyweight. He made his mark in the boxing arena. He was making a special appearance in his hometown, Salt Lake City. I was dumbfounded.

"I'll be damned."

Max Mellen and I weighed in at 125 pounds. Jack Dempsey made his formal introductions and when he called us to center ring, my heart skipped beats. It was awesome being so close to a legend.

The first round bell rung and I sprung to my feet and headed for the center of the ring. I had to use this first round as my opportunity to feel Mellen out, his fighting style and his strengths and weaknesses. He was light on his feet and kept away from me for the first round. By the fourth of this six-round bout Jack Dempsey was standing over him giving him the full ten count. I knocked him out with a strong right cross. Jack Dempsey held my right arm up high in the center of the ring and he declared me the winner by a knockout. I was thrilled. I won the fight and double thrilled that the Great Jack Dempsey announced my win.

Kid Davis came into the dressing room and praised me for a great fight and handed me seven dollars and fifty cents for the win. I was so in need of money I took it and put it in my pocket. If it were any other place or time I would have told him to give it to charity.

"Danny, I scheduled you to fight again next Monday night in the main event against Tony De Voe."

"Okay, Kid, I'll be there."

From my inquiries, Tony De Voe was an unknown boxer, so I was confused why Kid matched me with him in the main event. However, I trained hard the next week and felt in shape and ready for a main event. I won the last fight by a knockout and the great Jack Dempsey witnessed it.

Kid Davis kept his word and continued to let me train at his gym for nothing and I took full advantage of it. The manager at the Salvation Army maintained his loyalty and continued to feed and lodge us and we gave him tickets for the next bout.

Mutty became a seasoned corner man and his skill at taping my hands became perfect. He was the best man in my corner and the best friend in my life. We entered the ring for the main event and in the middle of the third round the referee counted to ten over Tony De Voe. A solid punch to his jaw put him away. Mutty and I were in the dressing room taking my gloves off when Kid Davis came in and congratulated me on a great fight. He handed me fifteen dollars. Wow, I laughed to myself and put the money in my pocket. I knew that I didn't have a choice. Mutty and I were in the bottom of a well trying to claw our way out.

"Danny, you're scheduled to fight Leroy Gibson next Monday night in the main event."

"Thanks, Kid, I'll be there."

I knew it had to get better. Kid was making money from the large attendance and my wins. The next payday had to get bigger. I stayed faithful to my workout ethic and trained hard for the upcoming fight. Mutty never lost his interest. He stood by me. He always made sure I had everything I needed.

Monday night came around fast. Mutty and I were in the dressing room taping my hands and putting my gloves on. The arena was filled to capacity and I said to Mutty, "Before you tape up my hands I want you to go to the ticket office and snoop around and see if you can find out what the ticket sales were so far tonight."

"You got it, Danny."

Leroy Gibson's past and present fight record was a mystery to me and Mutty. We didn't even know where he came from.

Mutty led me to the ring and lifted the ropes for me. I loosened up in my corner and waited for instructions. The ropes on the opposite side of the ring lifted and in stepped Leroy Gibson. He looked big and tough. After the referee's instructions, we went back to our corners. Gibson was even more threatening up close. The first round bell rung and Leroy beat me to the center of the ring. I circled him and dodged his jabs and punches. He made a few mistakes which allowed me hit him with a few hard jabs which stung him. In the fourth round, I put him down. The referee started his count and when he reached "six," Gibson was back on his feet. The fight went the six rounds distance. I won by decision. The crowd was on their feet giving me a standing ovation. I was popular on the street in the fight game because of my wins. Mutty removed my gloves, and like clockwork, Kid Davis made his appearance.

"Danny, what a performance. Great fight."

He handed me twenty dollars, and I knew at this point Kid Davis and Salt Lake City were history. I knew I was being used and my main reason for leaving New York was not to take anymore s——t from anybody.

"Mutty, what was the head count for this fight's ticket sales?"

"Danny, it was a record sellout 582 at last count."

"Kid, I want you to look me in the eyes and tell me what you see. Stare straight into my eyes."

Kid Davis began to pale and small tremors in his hands began to show signs of stress and being put on the spot.

"Danny London, one of the great featherweights of this time."

"Do I look like a chump or a fool to you, Kid?"

"Not at all, Danny. You're smart and a great professional boxer."

"And I'm a great businessman, now you lay two hundred and fifty dollars in my hand right now or I'm going to make you a candidate for a room at Salt Lake General."

Kid Davis was frozen, he couldn't move or talk, he peeled off the money from a large wad and put it in my hand. Mutty was in shock as he had never seen the street-smart side of his friend so cool and to the point.

It was time to move on and vacate Salt Lake City. That night back at the Salvation Army I told Mutty it was time to move on.

"It's time to get out of this farm country. We have a little money to take us further west and I think we should leave in the morning."

"I'm with you, Danny. Kid Davis used you and you had no choice but to do what you did, now it's our choice and it's time to leave."

We went down to see the manager and told him we were leaving town in the morning. I gave him ten dollars and thanked him. He was appreciative and said that we were welcome back anytime we were passing through.

"God bless and safe trip."

23

That night, Mutty and I went to the grocery store and bought some food for the trip. We went down to the freight yard and waited for the next freight heading west to arrive. The train came right on time. It crept down the tracks of the yard, and we jumped in the boxcar. We were becoming pros at entering and exiting the cars. I closed the door halfway and we were the only ones in the car. The freight train picked up speed and we felt safe and were glad we left Salt Lake City. We ate and laid our heads down allowing the choo-choo sound of the engine and the clacking of the wheels against the tracks to lull us into a deep sleep.

Mutty and I slept too long and the train was almost at a complete stop when we awoke. We started to panic knowing that the closer we got to the yard the greater the chance we would be caught by the yard bulls. They would take our stuff and money, probably beat us and possibly send us to jail. We quickly got to our feet and jumped off, practically running to the highway, afraid the bulls might be behind us. Luck was on our side this morning. We approached a highway sign, "Reno, Nevada, Two Miles." We walked to a gas station and cleaned up in the men's room. There was a diner next to the station and we ate tall stacks of pancakes and drank two cups of coffee. The meal cost thirty cents and it was worth a million dollars to our growling stomachs. When we left the diner it was around seven.

We walked to the middle of town and casinos lined the street. We were never in a gambling house before so we went inside and walked around. We watched the people playing blackjack, craps, roulette, and the slot machines. We were afraid to put even a nickel in a slot machine because we were so afraid to lose. Even though we didn't gamble, the sights we saw wandering around were amazing. People yelping when they won and cursing when they lost.

I guessed that people weren't worried about money in this city. It was a good place to try my luck boxing. I told Mutty that we needed to find a gym and see if I could get a fight and make some money. Mutty talked to a guy that worked in the casino and he gave him directions to a gym nearby where the matchmaker was a man named Clams. The gym was easy to find and Clams sat right inside the door dressed as a circus clown. He had a big gut, oversized pants held up by wide suspenders, and to complete the outfit, a big, red, bloodshot nose sat in the middle of his round face.

He asked lots questions about my record and was amazed that at eighteen I had so many fights and so many wins.

"How long will you be in Reno?"

I never looked at Mutty. "Three weeks."

"You can fight this Saturday night at the arena if you're ready."

"I'm ready. What time?"

"Be there by seven o'clock and you'll fight first at eight."

"Can I use the gym to train?"

"Be my guest, train to your heart's content."

After the fight was set, we went to find the local Salvation Army and let the manager know that we would be staying for a while. He was accommodating and said that he was a fight fan and would come to watch the fight. Mutty and I already liked Reno. The people we met so far were kind, but we both agreed that Clams seemed a little shady and most likely had a bit of larceny running through his veins.

The gym was not far from the Salvation Army and I used the distance between as my roadwork. The gym was not like any gym I trained at in New York even the gym in Salt Lake City was better equipped than Clams' place, but it had to do. While I punched the heavy bag Mutty walked up to me. "You fight Billy West Saturday night."

"What do you know about him?"

"He's a local favorite and has fought in some good fights. He's out of San Francisco."

I listened to Mutty while I continued to punch the bag. I was still in shape from Salt Lake City and ready for the bout.

Saturday night came and Mutty and I were in the dressing room chatting while he taped my hands. He put my gloves on and rubbed my neck and back to limber me up. They called for the first bout and we made our way to the ring. There was a good size crowd in the arena; the purse must be pretty fat.

Mutty lifted the ropes and I went to my corner. Billy West was already seated in his corner and he looked well conditioned and ready for the bout. The referee instructed us on the rules and we went to our corners.

The first round bell rung and Billy West came out slowly expecting me to be the aggressor, but I was patient and intently studied his gloves. He began jabbing but couldn't land a single punch.

I sensed his frustration. He became irritable and lost his focus. In the fifth round the referee counted to ten over him. Mutty and I went back to the dressing room followed by Clams.

"Very impressive, Danny London. You're a talented and classy pugilist."

He reached into his pocket and handed me nine dollars. I was furious inside. More than anything I wanted to smash his face and flatten his big blood shot nose. Instead, I took the money. I knew I was the underdog in Reno and broke. My time would come.

Clams scheduled me for a second and third fight. The second fight I won by knockout and was paid ten dollars and the third fight I won also with a knock out and was to be paid twelve dollars. Clams handed me ten dollars and said that he'd give me two dollars on Monday. Well, Monday never came because the next night, Mutty and I were inside a boxcar headed for San Francisco.

24

The freight cars chugged through the mountains of Nevada and Northern California. It was cold and damp and was taking forever to reach San Francisco. Mutty was curled up in the corner of the boxcar in a deep sleep like a bear hibernating during the winter. My eyes were wide open and I thought about the winning fights I had during the trip. They were great wins for me, solid knockouts.

I knew the money I received for the fights was peanuts, but I considered it as survival money. I knew the managers took advantage of me, but that was about to change. My father's face flashed in front of my eyes and his words echoed loud and clear. "Do you think it'll be any different there?"

I had to keep myself positive and believe that better fights and paydays were coming in California.

Mutty woke up and we ate some of the food we bought in Reno and we felt content and excited that we were almost at our destination. I cracked the door and saw that the sun was trying to burn through the thick clouds. It was late morning and the freight train was still traveling at high speed and not slowing down. Mutty and I began to wonder if we hopped the wrong train and were heading in the wrong direction. We just had to wait it out and see where the train ended up.

I was uncomfortable thinking we would pull into the freight yard in broad daylight. We would be sitting ducks waiting for the bulls to pick us off. The sun was almost straight up in the sky and the train started to slow. This was our opportunity to get ready to jump and hopefully land in San Francisco.

The freight yard was near the bay and many ships were docked at the Embarcadero according to a large sign. We jumped out and found a small eatery serving breakfast on the pier. Many longshoremen were enjoying their breakfast before their workday began and the place was packed. We had hot coffee, fried eggs, toast, and bacon. We asked the counter guy for directions to the Salvation Army.

"Yeah, it's easy. It's on the corner of Market and Valencia Street in the Mission District."

We thanked him, paid for our breakfast and headed to the Salvation Army.

When we left the diner the fog had lifted and the sun was warm. It was great to be outdoors. We walked to the center of the city looking for the Salvation Army. San Francisco was quaint and beautiful, the streets were clean, and the buildings had beautiful architecture.

It took us about half an hour to get to the Salvation Army and when we entered the building it was crowded, not like the farm towns where there weren't too many drifters. This was a city full of needy people who were down on their luck. Times were hard and people needed a hand to survive. We were a part of this scenario.

The people in charge were extremely overwhelmed trying to accommodate all the transients. They were helpful to each person, but people waited for hours to be called. Finally we were called and were given cots to sleep on and meal tickets for a local cafeteria. We took hot showers, cleaned up, and took a short nap. When we woke it was midafternoon and we decided to take a walk. We headed down Market Street and were enjoying the weather and the sights when we heard our names yelled out. We stopped short and whipped around, it was Joey Ray from Salt Lake City. We met him there while he was training in Kid Davis's Gym.

"What are you doing here?"

"Probably the same as you, looking for a fight that'll give us a decent payday."

"Maybe I can help you out. Follow me and I'll introduce you to someone who might be able to help."

Joey Ray took us to Joe Herman's Gym on Market Street. We entered the gym and the old familiar sweaty smell overwhelmed our nostrils. It was a sweet fragrance to me. The gym pulsed with life, the energy of the many boxers in training.

Joey Ray introduced me to Doc Miller. He told him I was a boxer he knew from Salt Lake City. Doc Miller was known as a big-time manager in San Francisco and also had a reputation of a high roller in the gambling world. Doc Miler was a thin, middle-aged man dressed in sporty clothes. When he shook my hand, I noticed how extremely large and strong his hand was.

He began asking me the typical questions about my age, weight, and fight record. He seemed interested after he heard my stats. He said that he would like to see me in the ring with his fighter, Little Dempsey.

"Fine with me."

Doc Miller yelled across the gym to the locker man to give me boxing gear, shoes, trunks, and gloves. Mutty, Joey, and I went into the dressing room. I changed and Mutty did a great job taping my hands and was concerned if I was ready to fight after our trip.

"How do you feel, Danny? Are you tired?"

"No, the nap helped me and I still feel strong from my workouts in Reno."

Mutty gave me a fast rubdown on my neck and shoulders and told me he found out that Little Dempsey is Filipino and scheduled to fight Johnny Pena in a main event next week. We left the dressing room and I went into the ring. I turned around and saw Little Dempsey jumping up and down to loosen up. He was stocky and muscular.

Doc Miller yelled, "Time!"

I went to the center of the ring and started jabbing lightly. Little Dempsey went crazy on me, slugging me nonstop all over. He gave me the ass kicking of my life. His punches were hurting me pretty bad.

"Time!"

In my corner I tried to catch my breath and compose myself. I thought about jab, jab, jab, and the right cross that served me so well up to this point. I needed to get back to my fight and fast.

"Time!"

When Doc Miller called time again, all the boxers in the gym gathered ringside to watch us fight. Now I was determined to box my fight and give Little Dempsey a lesson. He couldn't touch me in this round, but I landed punches that hurt him badly. His nose and mouth were bleeding profusely and he was finished in the second round. The boxers around the ring hooted and hollered for me. Doc

Miller walked briskly toward me with his face all screwed up. He started yelling at the top of his lungs. "You ruined my boxer. I don't know if he'll be able to fight next week."

"Well, Doc, he hurt me in that first round and I had to give it to him in the second. I ain't takin' no s——t. You wanted to see me fight."

Doc Miller was stuck for words and dropped his head and shook it. Quietly, he looked up at me.

"Okay, I'll get you a furnished room and you can train here every day on my dime."

He reached into his pocket and gave Mutty twenty-five dollars.

The furnished room Doc Miller arranged for us was clean and comfortable and not far from the gym. I worked out for the next week and Saturday night I watched Little Dempsey fight Jonny Pena in the main event. He lost in a close decision. Doc Miller said that the reason Little Dempsey lost was because he hasn't been right since I fought him.

I trained hard for the next two weeks and word was out about me. Doc Miller couldn't find anybody around the Bay Area who would fight me. They all heard I ruined Little Dempsey. I was disgusted and Mutty and me went to see Doc Miller.

"Doc, I can't hang around here for nothing, if you can't get me a fight then it's time for me to move on."

"I'm sorry, Danny. I tried but no one will fight you. I hate to see you go, but I understand if you do."

"We're going south to Los Angeles, maybe I can get some fights there."

We shook hands and remained friends and Doc Miller gave me twenty dollars for traveling money.

"Thank you very much, Doc. I'll never forget how you treated us while we were here."

"You're welcome, Danny, and if you ever get back this way just look me up."

Mutty and I woke up and it was still dark outside. We got our things together and went down to the truck stop and got a lift to San Jose. He dropped us off and said that he knew of a truck stop in San Jose where we possibly could get a lift further south. We did get a lift to Santa Barbara, a long ride in an old truck. We were hungry when we jumped out. We went to a diner and ate a good meal.

It was late morning when Mutty walked over to the coast highway and stuck out his thumb and hoped someone would pick us up and give us lift to Los Angeles. We stayed out on the highway less than an hour, when a new looking sedan stopped and the driver asked where we were going. Mutty answered that we were headed to Los Angeles.

"Well, I'm going to San Diego and I'll pass through Los Angeles. You guys are welcome to ride along."

Santa Barbara was a distance from Los Angeles. This guy probably wanted some conversation during the long trip. I sat in the back seat and enjoyed the beautiful scenery. The mountains, beaches, and ocean kept my interest during the ride. In the front, Mutty listened to the guy talk incessantly about everything.

"If you guys don't mind, I'm going to stop for a quick burger."

Mutty and I never turned down an opportunity to eat, so we joined him for a tasty burger, fries, and a cold drink. Surprisingly, the guy paid for our meal and we were grateful. We got back on the road and it was midafternoon when we finally arrived in Los Angeles. He dropped us off in the center of the city. We thanked him and he drove off.

As we walked, Mutty told me the guy was a queer.

"What the hell is a queer?"

"He likes to give men blow jobs."

"He's crazy, what the hell."

Mutty went to his knees and laughed hysterically until he was crying. Finally he stood up, looked at me, and shook his head.

25

Los Angeles had its share of people who were out of work just like the other cities we visited. As we walked down one of the main boulevards, bums laid on the sidewalk on pieces of cardboard boxes covered in dirty old blankets. As we approached they staggered over asking for spare change. They were filthy and stunk of whiskey.

"We're not working. We don't have any money."

They continued one after another coming right up in our faces begging for money for whiskey. Finally, we practically ran across the street and went into a deli and ordered two sandwiches. We walked and found a nearby park, sat on the bench, and ate our food. Our stomachs were satisfied, so we decided to see more of the city.

"Danny, let's go to Hollywood, I've heard so much about it."

We went to the corner and leaped on a trolley car and we went for a wonderful ride through the streets of Los Angeles to Hollywood. We jumped off at Hollywood Boulevard and walked around looking at the beautiful homes. We went to Sunset Boulevard and Santa Monica Boulevard and they were terrific places to visit.

It was getting late and we needed to locate the Jewish Federation to see if they would put us up for the night. We headed back to downtown Los Angeles and easily found the Jewish Federation building. We went inside and an elderly rabbi approached us. Mutty was prepared with a story.

"Can I help you, young men?"

"We're from New York and we're trying to get back home. Our transportation tickets haven't arrived yet and we wondered if your organization could assist us with a meal and a room for the night?"

The rabbi was accommodating and wrote an address on a piece of paper and told us to go there and say that Rabbi Rubin sent us.

We thanked him, left the building, and walked for about a mile to the address. It was a Jewish home where they fed us and gave us a room for the night. The food was hot and so was the shower, which made our travel-worn bodies feel refreshed. We were on top of the world knowing we would be safe for the night.

We woke the next morning after a restful night's sleep. We ate a delicious breakfast then headed downtown looking for a gym. It was easy to find and we welcomed the old sweaty smell. It was packed with starving hopeful boxers. They were training hard in hopes of landing a fight that would line their pockets with money.

There had to be more than a hundred boxers in the gym. Again, I saw my dad's face and heard his haunting words. "Do you think it's going to be better there?"

He was right. My mind raced. I felt discouraged and furious at myself for dragging Mutty along on this profitless trip. I looked at Mutty and motioned him to follow me out of the gym.

"I'm sorry I got you involved in my craziness. I thought we could do well out here and it's a nightmare. I won't find my dream here."

"Danny, I'm a big boy, you never twisted my arm or held me hostage. We tried, it didn't work, there's no shame. We'll get a job and make enough to get back home. You'll get your dream and I'll be right by your side when you do."

We looked for jobs as dishwashers and we went down to the bus station to see if we could change flat tires. We even tried the bootblack business, but there was nothing. Times were as bad in this part of the country as the rest, thousands of people out of work. We had no luck finding work. We were disgusted and depressed.

"Mutty, we need to get out of this town and go back home."

"I'm ready and want to get back home to New York. Let's go."

We put all our money together and went to the grocery store and bought food for the trip back east. We went to the freight yard and waited for the sun to set. It was near midnight when the freight train slowly ambled down the track and we jumped into the boxcar, I closed the door halfway and we went to sleep. We were heading to Yuma, Arizona. We were seasoned veteran hobos jumping in and out of boxcars and traveling across the country. Traveling by boxcar was adventurous and risky, not knowing exactly who you were going to meet. Maybe the bulls would be waiting for you when you jumped off and they'd rob and beat you. You could end up in jail. But we were young and desperate trying to make a future for ourselves.

It was daylight when the train slowed. I shook Mutty out of a deep sleep. He was a testimonial to our boxcar accommodations. He slept like he was home in his own bed.

"Where are we?"

"We're in Yuma, Arizona."

The sun was warm and the red desert sand ran for many miles to the mountains off in the distance. The train slowed to about ten miles an hour and our feet hit the desert sand. We walked to the highway where a sign read we were five miles from Yuma. Just off the highway there was a beautiful valley with an apple orchard and an orange grove. The apples and oranges were ripe and low hanging. Mutty and I jumped over the wooden fence surrounding the grove and started eating the fruit.

The apples tasted so sweet and the orange juice dripped off our chins. We picked and loaded the fruit into our jackets. We looked like two potbelly stoves when we climbed back over the fence. We stumbled back to the highway loaded down with fruit when a police car pulled up. An officer wearing a large white cowboy hat got out of his car and approached.

"What do you boys have in your coats?"

Mutty opened his coat and all the fruit fell out hitting the ground and I followed suit.

"My God, you stole from the farmer, now y'all pick up the fruit and put it back where it belongs."

We followed the officer's orders. He waited for us to get back over the fence.

"Okay, now get in the back seat of my cruiser."

We rode for a while and the officer never said a word to us. We were sure we were on our way to jail for stealing apples and oranges. He drove us down a long dirt road and turned into a side road with a sign that hung over an entrance, THE TRANSIENT BOYS CAMP.

He told us to get out of the car and he led us inside the building. He motioned us to sit. He knocked on a door marked Supervisor's Office. The door opened and a man in his forties looked at us.

The officer went in and we heard him talking to the supervisor, but we couldn't make out what he was saying. After a few minutes the officer walked out, right past us, without a word or a glance, and left the building.

The supervisor waved us into his office and told us to sit.

"Where you boys from?"

"New York, and we were trying to get back home."

The supervisor drilled us on what we were doing here so far from home.

"You boys will stay here until your parents can provide you with transportation funds to go back to New York."

Mutty and I took a deep breath. We were not going to jail. The supervisor was calm and not at all abusive.

"You'll both work here, maybe washing dishes in the mess hall or other chores. You'll be paid ninety cents a week and get room and board."

He took us to the mess hall and we ate and ate like two starving jungle lions. He smiled and told us that if we wanted more it was there, but we couldn't fit another bite into our bellies. He took us to the barracks where everyone was in bed and sleeping. He told us that lights out was ten o'clock. He gave us blankets, sheets, pillows, and clean towels. We washed and went to sleep.

There were no problems while we stayed there and everyone treated us well. The next morning we woke and the boys in the barracks introduced themselves. They ranged in age from twelve to eighteen and were from all parts of the country.

The supervisor, Mike, entered the barracks and handed Mutty and me new matching blue work pants and shirts. Every boy at the camp wore the identical uniform. The clothes fit just right and we thanked Mike and followed the rest of the camp boys to the mess hall and ate a fine breakfast. Mutty and I along with a few other boys went into the kitchen and began to wash dishes.

Every one of the boys worked hard and they made it fun by joking with each other. They all knew their jobs, so no one had to be told what to do. The work schedule was only three hours a day and the rest of the day we spent involved in camp activities.

We all left the kitchen and went outside. The morning air was fresh and clean. The camp had a baseball field, a basketball court, and a football field. There was a gym for wrestling and to my surprise a fully equipped boxing facility.

The boxing ring was tournament size. The gym had a speed bag, a heavy bag, and all the equipment to train for boxing. My eyes grew wide and twinkled like stars. Everything was brand new. I put on a pair of boxing gloves and started out on the speed bag and then skipped rope. When I finished, I looked up and saw Mike standing in the doorway intently watching me.

"Danny, you're a boxer?"

"Yes, Mike, I've had some professional fights."

"Every Saturday evening we put on a boxing show for the camp and folks from the community come to see the bouts. You would do me a great favor by putting on an exhibition Saturday. It would be appreciated by the camp kids and the community."

"I'll do whatever you ask and if you need a substitute for a bout I'll do it."

"Thanks for the offer, Danny, but I'm sure these boxers aren't of your caliber."

Mike left chuckling to himself.

I worked out for the rest of the afternoon and the day passed by quickly. Working out felt great, it was just what I needed. I went back to the mess hall and ate a delicious meal with Mutty; I was hungry. With our bellies full, we went to the kitchen and washed the supper dishes and cleaned up the counters.

After supper, there were even more activities offered to the boys. There was a reading room with a library, an art room supplied with all the tools to paint and sculpt, and a music room with a jukebox and pool table. Mutty and I went to the music room and sat quietly on the couch listening to music while we watched several boys shoot pool on a regulation table.

Everyone walked around feeling happy and safe, the boys supported each other, it was amazing that we felt this way considering we were forced here. I thought about the police officer who put us in the back seat of his car and drove us to the camp. We could be in a jail cell for stealing fruit from the farmer's orchard. He was the reason Mutty and I were at the camp and not rotting in a jail cell. Mutty glanced at me and winked. "Danny, come with me."

Mutty took me into the kitchen, opened the freezer, and took out some ice cream. He scooped out heaping portions and filled our bowls and we enjoyed a sweet treat.

We cleaned up our mess, returned to the barracks, and fell off to sleep.

The next morning we ate another delicious healthy breakfast, completed our chores in the kitchen, and then headed over to the gymnasium. Many of the boys followed us after they heard that I was a boxer. Mike stood by as Mutty and I began to teach a few boys some basic boxing skills. We worked with them all day and Mutty and I felt like boxing instructors. Mike was so happy with us he walked away smiling from ear to ear.

The first week at the camp flew by. We were so busy that we never once thought about time. Saturday morning during breakfast Mike handed an envelope containing ninety cents to each boy. The look on their faces made you think they received ninety dollars. Everyone appreciated every penny but most of all we appreciated how well we were treated—as respectful young men, not as hoodlums.

Mike asked Mutty and me to come to his office after we finished our chores in the kitchen. We knew we didn't break any rules, so we wondered what he wanted. We knocked on the door and entered.

"You have done a great job here. You took the lead and unselfishly gave your time to the boys. To show you that I appreciate your leadership, I'm giving you a pass and bus fare to spend the day in Yuma. Be back by three o'clock."

Mike took us off guard and we were grateful and thanked him for his generosity. We headed out the main road and caught the bus to Yuma. The scenery was so different than from a subway ride in New York. The desert sun was hot and strong. It was funny, we were free and blessed, and we caught a break and were surrounded by people who genuinely cared about our well being for the first time in a long while.

Yuma was a small, quiet city with not too much to see of interest. We walked around and saw an old Indian sitting on the corner with a feather stuck in his hair. We had a bowl of chili and a taco in a family-run café. We were back at the camp by two thirty.

Mike saw us walk into the building and thanked us for coming back on time.

"Tonight we scheduled six bouts. The boys are wild with excitement knowing that Danny London is putting on an exhibition of boxing skills."

Over two hundred people sat in attendance. Mutty refereed the six bouts, and I demonstrated boxing techniques and skills in the ring. I received a round of applause from the boys.

The days at the camp flew by and we stayed interested and involved. We did our chores and took part in the activities the camp offered. Three weeks passed when Mike called us into his office.

"Your transportation tickets have arrived and you're scheduled to leave for New York in the morning."

He handed us our tickets. Actually, we were saddened by the news. We made friends and felt we had accomplished something worthwhile. We knew that everyone at some time had to leave the camp and we were ready to get home, but we still felt a little down by the news.

The next morning at breakfast we said our good-byes and wished everyone well. Mike took us to the Yuma train depot where the passenger train was on the tracks waiting.

We started to feel sad and down about leaving. Mike gave us both big hugs and solid handshakes for good luck.

He let us know we'd be missed at the camp, but it was time to get back to our lives and get on track. There were marvelous experiences waiting for us.

"Mike, we don't know how to thank you for all you've done for us."

"I do hope I'll see you again someday."

We boarded the train and while it slowly pulled away from the station we waved good-bye to Mike through the window.

"Mutty, I'll never forget that guy. He's the greatest guy I ever met. Look at us sitting here like kings instead of hobos hopping boxcars and risking our lives. I'm never going to jump on another freight train. It takes too damn long to get anywhere."

We shook hands and laughed our asses off. The train took three and half days to get to New York, but the accommodations were so much better than the dirty boxcars. We ate decent meals and slept in clean, comfortable births. At last, the train pulled into Grand Central Station. We were elated, hugging and laughing. We vowed to remain friends for life.

"Here we are, New York, happy to be back."

26

Mutty and I were like kids waking up on Christmas morning, everything made us happy now that we were home safe and sound. Mutty took the subway to Brooklyn and I went home to Coney Island. My family greeted me with opened arms. It was a warm welcome home.

"Dad, you were right. I learned a lesson I had to find out for myself."

"You'll be smarter next time when you get an urge to go and think that the grass is greener somewhere else."

I went to my bedroom and thought about the wisdom in my dad's words. He was an intelligent man who was full of love for his children. I undressed, shaved, and took a long, hot shower. I dressed in my sport clothes and sat down to enjoy a mouth-watering meal with the family. I looked at Mom, who, no matter what was going on in life, figured out a way to make our home a warm, inviting place where we were safe from the harsh world.

"Mom, there's no place like home."

It was early in the evening and I got the urge to go and see my good friend, Al Tesh. I wanted to let him know that

I was back. I went to his house, knocked and he answered, "You're back."

He picked me up like he did so often, swirled me around and kissed my cheek. He was thrilled to see me. He missed me.

"You've gained some weight and look stronger."

"Yeah I'm feeling strong." I rolled up my shirt sleeve and made a muscle.

We laughed and I realized how much I missed him.

We spent a couple hours together and I told him all about me and Mutty's nonprofitable but adventurous trip. I talked while Al listened with his mouth wide open, surprised at some of the stories. It got pretty late and I left telling Al that we'd get together again real soon. I returned home and was glad to sleep in my own bed.

I got back into a light routine of roadwork. On the way home one day I stopped at the local newsstand and picked up a paper. The headlines read "Al Peters, Kings County Amateur Boxing Champion, Shot Dead!" Al was a good friend who got mixed up with the wrong people. I thought about the day he helped me get my amateur card. I went to his services and remembered the good times I shared with him. I lost a good friend.

I started to work out at Stillman's Gym again. I worked out hard during the day and went to bed early each night. I was dead serious about getting into great shape. One morning, Irving Cohen, manager of Rocky Graziano, middleweight champion of the world, approached me.

"Danny, how have you been?"

"Fine, been away for awhile but I'm back. I'm training hard and in tip top shape."

"Are you under contract with anybody?"

"No, I've learned my lesson about signing long-term contracts. They never worked for me."

"Why don't you let me manage you? I'll get you the fights that will get you decent money."

Along with Rocky Graziano, Irving managed many good boxers. I had heard through the grapevine that he was honest with his boxers, but I was naïve in the past and have been burned too many times.

"Sounds good, but like I said, I'm not signing any more contracts."

"How about I manage you and get you some fights without a contract, and you judge how we work out."

It sounded like a good deal and I knew that Irving Cohen had connections to schedule legitimate fights with up and coming boxers. I agreed with one stipulation, we would agree on a fight-by-fight basis where I was told the purse up front. Irving and I shook hands and soon after I had many fights in Brooklyn and out of town.

Things went well. Irving lived up to the bargain, I knew the purses beforehand and the money was decent. Irving hired different trainers each time I was scheduled to fight. I wasn't too confident with this training method, because I faced different methods with each new trainer. I liked knowing my trainers. I was happy with Whitey Bimstein and Ray Arcel and sometimes Irving would hire them, but for only that fight.

Irving booked a fight in Montreal with the featherweight champion of Canada, Dave Castilloux. Irving hired Whitey Bimstein and Ray Arcel to train me and we traveled to Montreal. They got me in terrific shape and I was ready for the ten-round bout. Castilloux was strong and tough and an excellent puncher, and he could take a punch. I continued my constant jabs in every round. In the tenth, after a barrage of jabs, I hit him with my right cross and he was ready to go down wobbling on his feet when the bell saved him. I lost by a decision and I knew he got the hometown wave.

I went back to Coney Island and rested for a few days. My family knew the results of the Castilloux fight by listening to every round on the radio. My father knew I was down.

"Patience, Danny, you'll be the champ one day."

It was 1932 and Benny Lenard, a one-time lightweight champion of the world, was trying to make a comeback and regain the title. Whitey Bimstein and Ray Arcel worked him hard; he needed to lose weight. I was in Stillman's training hard and sparring with anyone who would jump in the ring with me. Lenard stopped his training and came over to watch. The next day Whitey told me that Lenard wanted to spar with me.

"Whitey, Lenard outweighs me by a ton, he'll murder me."

"Lenard likes the way you box, you have the speed that he lacks. He wants to use your speed to help him get into shape, he's not interested in punching your lights out."

I agreed and the next day I was in the ring with Lenard.

We went ten rounds and Lenard never put a glove on me. His goal was to increase his speed to prepare for his fight against Jimmy McClarnin for the championship. On the road back to regain his title Lenard won every fight.

When he finally fought against McClarnin, McClarnin stopped him. Lenard hung up his gloves after the fight. He was too old to start training again, so he became a radio

Danny London

announcer for boxing in Ridgewood Grove, Brooklyn, for the Saturday night fights.

When Lenard heard that I was scheduled to fight Al Cuillo, one of the toughest southpaws in boxing, at the Ridgewood Grove Arena, he came to see me at Stillman's Gym.

"Danny, I would like to repay the favor. Remember how you helped me out in the ring as my sparring partner? Al Cuillo is dangerous. He has a deadly punch for a southpaw. I want to work with you and show you the techniques used to fight a southpaw."

Lenard worked with me every day for a week. I listened and followed his every instruction. I took advantage of his knowledge and was grateful for it. Whitey and Ray were with us every step of the way. They were impressed with Lenard's knowledge of southpaw boxers and his pointers to block Cuillo's deadly punch.

That Saturday we left the dressing room at Ridgewood Grove Arena, Whitey on one side of me and Ray on the other. This was a big fight for my manager, Irving Cohen, and me. He was shaking like a dog s—— razor blades.

Whitey lifted the ropes and I entered the ring. I looked over at Lenard who was the radio announcer for the fight. He winked and I winked back.

I was loosening up when the ring announcer introduced the boxers. We went to the center of the ring and the referee gave us our instructions.

The bell rung and I moved to the center of the ring and started circling to the left side of him. I hooked him in the ribs several times. I threw jabs to his jaw and then sent a right cross to his head.

I continued this strategy in every round and in the fifth again I circled to the left jabbing his ribs and jabbing his jaw.

When the timing was right I hit him with a solid right cross to the left eye and blood spurted out and ran down his eye and face. The laceration was deep and the referee stopped the fight.

I was the underdog in the fight and I was pleased with the way I handled myself. My training paid off, I couldn't believe it. The bookies and bettors lost big money betting against me. I went over to Cuillo's corner and shook his hand and apologized for cutting his eye so badly. He commented that it was a good fight and the best fighter won.

I was in the dressing room getting the gloves taken off when Lenard ran in and gave me a hug congratulating me for an excellent fight. I thanked him for taking time out of his schedule to work with me.

"Don't mention it."

A couple of months later I heard Lenard quit radio announcing and became a referee at Saint Nickolas Arena. At a main event in the arena, Benny Lenard had a heart attack in the ring and died. I was devastated when I heard the news and cried all night. He was a great fighter and even a greater human being; a sincere gentleman who I had the honor to know.

Six months passed and Irving Cohen said that things were slowing down. I told him that it was time for me to move on. He understood, shook my hand, and wished me luck.

Al Weil, manager for Rocky Marciano, heavyweight champion of the world, wanted to manage me. I went with him and he scheduled a couple of fights. I wasn't too satisfied or impressed with him and we soon parted. I decided to lay low for a while and get some needed rest.

Time passed rapidly. All I did each day was roadwork on the boardwalk. One day at home a visitor came to see me, my old friend, Salvatore, from sign reading school who I hadn't seen in a couple of years. I was glad to see him and invited him in. My mother made us coffee and served us cake. We talked about our days in sign school.

"The reason I came to see you is on Saturday night there's a dance sponsored by the Deaf Club Association. Many kids from the old school will be there."

I thought about it for a minute and knew that I wanted to see some of my old classmates. It would be a good time. I wasn't training for a fight, so it was time for enjoyment. I thanked Salvatore for taking the time to come to Coney Island and invite me.

"I'll be there Saturday night at eight sharp."

"Great, it'll be lots of fun."

Salvatore left and I began to get excited about seeing old friends. I wanted a change from my normal routine.

27

Saturday night arrived and I cleaned up and put on my new suit. I felt great and thought about the classmates I would see after all these years. I couldn't remember the last time that I socialized with friends. It would be a radical change from the circle of boxing folks that were in my life.

I entered the living room and my mom whistled and grinned. "Where are you going, Danny?"

I told her about Salvatore's visit and invitation to the Deaf Club Dance. "Can't wait to see my classmates, I wonder if many of them will remember me."

"I think they'll remember Danny London and the infamous pointer."

We both chuckled.

"Have a good time and enjoy yourself."

I walked with a bounce in my step to the subway and went to Lexington Avenue in Manhattan to the Deaf Club Association building. I walked upstairs and saw a banner hung across the entrance.

  WELCOME, DANNY LONDON
  GUEST OF HONOR

Salvatore pulled a fast one on me. What the hell was going on, guest of honor? I walked inside and the room was filled with people, some I recognized and some strangers. When they saw me, they applauded and ran over and surrounded me. They hugged me, slapped my back, and shook my hand. Wow, what a reception, I was amazed.

After a while the crowd thinned out and I could breathe and walk around. With the signing and lip reading that was going on, it was like a comedy show. I was proud of myself, I was signing like a pro with everyone until my fingers began to stiffen from being out of signing practice and signing nonstop for a long time. I kept going though. I didn't want to miss a conversation.

Salvatore and I were talking and enjoying the music and the night. Out of nowhere two hands covered my eyes in an attempt for me to guess who it was. The palms of the person's hands were small and smooth and a sensational aroma of fine perfume engulfed me. I slowly turned and to my surprise it was Harriet with her fiery glowing red hair matching her perfectly painted red lips. We hugged and she gave me a kiss on the cheek resembling the kiss from many years ago.

Harriet introduced me to the very good-looking fellow she was with. Harriet signed, "Danny, this is Lance, we're engaged to be married."

Lance extended his hand and spoke clearly with perfect English. Harriet was extremely intelligent and found the man of her dreams.

I wished them good luck in their futures and they in return wished me good luck with my career. We parted and Harriet and Lance headed for the dance floor and I continued my conversation with Salvatore.

A jazz band played and I relaxed, listening to the soothing sound. People danced even though they couldn't hear the music. They felt the vibrations through the floor and they never missed a beat. The jazz band played for thirty minutes and then took a fifteen-minute break throughout the night.

I felt a tap on my shoulder; I turned and was greeted by Josephine, a classmate. We hugged and kissed hello. I blushed a bit and felt funny for some reason, I don't know why. I signed that I was glad to see her again. We talked about how long it's been and some of the fun times we shared in school. I was so glad I remembered how to sign. Josephine came to the dance with a girlfriend.

"Danny I want you to meet my friend Muriel."

I signed, "Happy to meet you." She signed back that she was glad to finally meet me. Muriel grabbed my shoulder, pulled me down, and yelled *Hello* right into my ear. My ear buzzed. I thought she made me go deaf again. I controlled myself and told her that I could hear and speak. Muriel was deaf but after her hello, I wasn't surprised she had her voice.

When my ear finally stopped humming, I took a good look at Muriel. She was beautiful, petite, with intense deep blue eyes. She looked at me in a mysterious way with her eyes burning through me. I wanted to get to know her better and I felt like she was feeling the same way. The band started to play a slow soft jazzy beat and I asked her if she'd like to dance. Again she almost blew out my restored hearing.

"Yes, I'd love to dance."

I bent over to her ear and in a soft voice I explained that I could hear her if she just spoke normally.

We danced together until the band took another break. I thanked her for the dances and she walked back to her girlfriend and I walked over to where Salvatore and the other guys were hanging out. The guys and I talked about boxing and I was the center of attraction. The evening flew by and before I knew it the last tune was played and it was time to leave.

Salvatore and I walked around saying good-bye to everyone and then we took the subway home. I thanked Salvatore for the surprise and a great evening.

"Good luck, Danny, and when you fight again, look in the crowd, I'll be there rooting for you."

We shook hands and I went home. I was tired, happily tired from an amazing night with friends, standing on my feet, signing, and dancing. These were new exercises for me. I slept soundly all night.

My days were routine, working out at Stillman's Gym and roadwork on the boardwalk to stay in ready to box shape. My manager, Al Weil, promoted a fight with Leo Dazzo, a good fighter with an excellent record. The venue for the fight was Ebbets Field, home of the Brooklyn Dodgers.

The night of the fight, the ring was set up in the infield with seats for people around the ring and in the stands of the stadium. It was a grueling six-round fight. I believed I was ahead of Leo Dazzo on points. I got robbed and lost by decision.

The outcome was unpopular with the fans and they went wild, booing and throwing things into the ring, but it didn't change anything and I was down and out.

In the dressing room Al said that he sent a message to Leo Dazzos' manager for a return match. Patiently, we waited, but no word came back. Now I was even more furious and bewildered. Why were these upsets always happening to me? I knew Al was just as pissed as me.

"Better luck next time."

He told me that the purse was one hundred fifty dollars. As usual, I got robbed twice that night, once by the scorers and now by Al. I took my cut and we left the stadium. On the street, Salvatore was waiting as promised. He was with his girlfriend and Muriel. With a warm smile she looked at me with her piercingly beautiful eyes.

"Did you see the fight?"

"We were too late. The darn subway wasn't on time. Did you win?"

"No, lost by a decision."

"Danny, I'm sorry. I hope I can see you fight next time."

Everyone hugged and said their good-byes and started to leave when Muriel turned back.

"See you again some time."

I went back over to Al and he drove me home. It was a sullen ride. I felt bad about everything that happened. My parents were waiting for me. They knew the results of the fight; they listened on the radio. My father was ready to greet me with his encouraging words.

"Don't worry and don't let this discourage you."

I knew my dad meant well, but I was sick of hearing the same old b——t that things were going to get better. When?

"I need to win, the more I win the more money I make."

I gave them the money as usual and went to bed.

I was down in the pits and had a sour taste in my mouth from the decision. I knew I had to dissolve these bad feelings, and I did. The next day I was back on the boardwalk doing roadwork and in Stillamn's Gym working out. Two weeks later, Al matched me up with Vic Caggiano in a six-round bout at Saint Nickolas Arena.

I worked out even harder for this fight. I didn't want the same thing that happened with the Dazzo fight to happen again. Saint Nickolas was a great venue for me; many friends and family from Coney Island would be in the stands cheering me on. Whitey talked to me while he taped my hands and put on the gloves and Ray rubbed my shoulders to keep me loose. They both told me to stay away from his right hand and fight my fight.

I entered the ring and the announcer introduced us. The crowd was alive and roaring. The referee instructed us on the rules and we went to our corners. The bell rung and for six rounds I gave Vic Caggiano boxing lessons, that in the future, would make him quiver every time he heard my name. I knew I was way ahead on points when the announcer walked center ring.

"Winner by decision, Caggiano."

The arena was silenced for a second, and then all hell broke loose. The crowd couldn't be contained. They went crazy, booing, cursing, and throwing bottles and chairs into the ring trying to hit the referee and the ring announcer. The cops jumped into the ring trying to shelter Caggiano and me from getting hit. They got us out of the ring and covered us all the way to our dressing rooms.

I sat on the rubdown table and Whitey screamed while he removed my gloves.

"Three f—— blind mice judges, three assholes."

My head hung low. I fought the fight with pure precision, like a technician, how could they be so blind?

A hand rested on my shoulder and I looked up and saw Hymie Miller.

"Cheer up, Danny. Great fight. Come by and see me."

I was so happy he saw the fight.

I still heard the roar of the crowd protesting the decision. They were massacring the arena, destroying every inch. Half an hour passed and the ring announcer slithered back in the ring and said that a giant mistake was made. The judges changed their ruling. Danny London won by reverse decision. Hymie Miller ran back into the dressing room and gave me the news.

I couldn't believe my ears. I never heard of a reverse decision and remembered immediately the Dazzo fight. It should have been a reverse decision.

"Well it's about time they did something right."

The crowd's booing changed to cheers. They were exhilarated and probably felt they were instrumental in the judges' decision. They left the arena chanting my name. Al handed me sixty dollars. Robbed again. I grinned so wide, two reasons, I won and this was the last time Al will pull a fast one on me.

I left the arena with all my friends and we stopped at a local bar to celebrate. When I entered, the people went wild. They carried me around on their shoulders and yelled, "The next champ!"

No one in the bar ever heard of a reverse decision and said that history was made in the boxing world tonight and the decision must be recorded in the official record book. Glasses were raised and the bartender handed me a glass of whiskey.

"I don't drink, but I'll toast with a glass of Coke."

I stayed until closing celebrating my win. I went home and slept soundly till morning. Even though I won my routine never changed. I was back doing my roadwork and training in the gym. I was determined to be a better fighter and someday have a chance at the title.

John J. Morabito

It was late Saturday afternoon when Al and I left the gym and were on our way home. I told him I'd see him tomorrow and he went toward his house and I crossed the street. On the opposite corner I saw Muriel standing a block away from my house.

"What in the world are you doing here?"

She smiled with her gorgeous blue steel eyes.

"I've been waiting three hours to see you. I wanted to say hello."

28

"Muriel, you shouldn't have come all the way out here to see me, you better go home."

Muriel's deep blue eyes filled with tears. She was hurt and I made her feel bad. I had to stay focused on training and fighting and I didn't need a girl in my life. I had no time for a relationship.

"I came to see you and I thought maybe you wanted to see me. The night at the school when we danced, the way you looked at me made me feel that you wanted to see me."

I put my arms around her and gave her a light hug.

"Wait here for me, I'll be right back."

She waited and had no idea where I was going. I left in a slow jog. I was one block away from my house. I ran inside and told my parents that I wouldn't be home for supper because I had an appointment.

I ran into my bedroom, took off my shirt, went in the bathroom, and washed my face and combed my hair. I put on a clean shirt and sprinted out of the house and back to see Muriel. Muriel stood and waited and when she saw me, she smiled and her blue eyes twinkled. She was beautiful and was interested in me.

Instantly, Muriel's hand grasped mine and we went for a walk on the boardwalk. The ocean air was refreshing and the sun was descending behind the horizon leaving a glow on the water.

"Are you hungry?"

"I haven't eaten since lunchtime."

I noticed her voice was quietly sweet. She no longer yelled and I loved talking to her.

We stopped at Nathan's Frankfurter Diner on the boardwalk. It wasn't fancy but it was cozy and we could still see the ocean from our seats. We ate tasty frankfurters with ice-cold lemonade. Muriel had no trouble keeping the conversation going. I learned about her likes and dislikes. She wasn't shy at all.

The sun made its final descent below the horizon when we left the diner. I softly held Muriel's hand as I walked her to the subway station. She sat close to me on the train and her warm body felt good next to mine. We never let go of each other's hand. It was if we were attached for life. We exited the train at her stop and I walked her home.

"When will I see you again, Danny?"

I was stuck for an answer. My words fumbled across my lips. She smiled and answered her own question.

"I know you're busy training and trying to be the best boxer you can. I don't want to distract you from your goal. I just like you and want to see you again."

"I'll keep in touch and we'll see each other soon."

I kissed her lightly on her cheek and she turned and went in her house. I knew as I walked back to the subway that I didn't sound convincing. In my heart, I wanted to see her again. I liked her too and she made me feel wonderful when I was close to her. When I kissed her I felt uneasy like

I do before the first round bell rings. I didn't know how to act with a girl; I was never in a relationship before. Muriel was emotional and I was never one to show my emotions.

I jumped back into my routine, daily roadwork and training at Stillman's. Whitey worked me hard and Al tried to match me up with a good fight.

Two weeks went by and on my way home from the gym, one block away from my house, waiting on the exact corner as before, stood Muriel. I became a statue and froze solid in my shoes. What does this girl want from me?

I approached her and her composure told me she was afraid to speak. Maybe she was sorry that she made the trip. After a moment of silence, she looked up at me and said that she hadn't heard from me and she just wanted to see me. I felt it took a lot of courage for her to say that and I felt bad that I hadn't contacted her after our evening. She stood on her tiptoes and kissed my cheek.

"I'm sorry I came, but I wanted to see you again, please don't be upset."

What was I doing? I liked Muriel a lot and down deep I was elated to see her, so why was I acting like I wasn't? What was wrong with me? She started to turn away and walk.

"Would you like to come to my house and meet my family?"

Her deep blues widened, the eyes I knew now I missed.

"I would like that very much."

I took Muriel's hand and walked home. My family had no idea she was coming, but still their reactions floored me. My brothers and sisters gave her dirty looks and my parents were downright cold to her. Surprisingly, my mother invited her to stay for dinner and we ate a spaghetti and meatball dinner, and had cake and tea for dessert. It was extremely awkward at the table. No one talked, very unusual for my family. I couldn't figure out why they were acting so strange.

Muriel thanked my mother and said that it was nice to meet everyone. We left and walked and talked on the boardwalk, and then I took Muriel to the train and back to her house. Our conversation was easy. I could talk to her like a friend. I was comfortable by her side and I cared for her and I felt she cared for me.

We stood in front of her house and I looked at her.

"I'm going away for a while and I won't be able to see you."

Tears came down her cheeks like Niagara Falls.

"I don't care, Danny, I'll wait for you"

She turned and ran to the top of the stairs. She was crying uncontrollably.

"Good-bye."

She vanished inside the door.

Slowly, I walked away. I was upset that she cared so much for me, and selfishly I was too involved in the world of boxing to even think about that kind of relationship. In a daze, I had to decide if I wanted Muriel to be a part of my life or should I end our relationship. I went to bed forcing Muriel from my thoughts.

I worked out with a vengeance this week at Stillman's Gym and ran on the boardwalk until my heart was ready to explode. I needed to keep my focus on boxing. Whitey told me Al wanted to see me in his office. I cleaned up and went to Al's office.

"Danny, Tony Canzoneri, the lightweight champion of the world, has requested that you to go to his camp and spar with him."

"Al, he's too big for me. It won't be a contest."

"Tony needs your speed to move around the ring with him. He'll pay you for your time."

"Sounds like a deal, I'll do it."

Two days later, Al and I left Manhattan and drove up the shore of the Hudson River to the town of Marlboro, New York, to Tony's training camp. On the trip up, the autumn scenery was magnificent. The mountainside trees were exploding with vibrant colors.

When we arrived, Al introduced me to Tony Canzoneri and his trainer, Lou Fink, one of the best trainers in the business.

There were two other sparring mates present, Willie Nussbaum and Pete Gallute, who I knew from Stillman's Gym. Tony was scheduled to fight Harry Dubinsky, a tough and skilled fighter from Chicago. The fight at Ebbets Field was advertised all over the city.

Tony's camp was equipped with the best training equipment and the accommodations were first class. The next day we started to spar with Tony. Willie and Pete went in the ring before me. Lou Fink wanted to save me for last, because he said that I had more speed than them.

"Danny, I want you to spar with Tony the same way that Willie and Pete did. Continually move around and jab. Use your speed and make Tony come after you."

I did what Lou asked and kept moving and jabbing, then Tony came too close and I jabbed him on the nose, which left a small cut. Lou yelled, "Time!"

Lou went over to him and checked his nose. I stayed in my corner, worried and scared that I f—— up. I didn't mean it, natural boxing instinct. Lou stopped the sparring for a couple of days to give Tony's nose a chance to heal. We continued with the roadwork and gym training. Lou was an excellent cut man and Tony's nose was back to normal in three days and we were back in the ring sparring to get Tony faster on his feet and ready to fight Dubinsky. By the third week Tony and the rest of us were in top shape.

One night after a grueling day of training, Tony, Willie, Pete, and I took a walk through the woods to the small town of Marlboro. It was quaint, only one small general store. Tony treated us to ice cream and on the way back to camp, they kidded around, talking about sex and the women they left behind and longed to see. I just laughed pretending I understood what they were talking about. I did find myself thinking about Muriel.

We went back to the playroom and Willie and Tony racked up the billiard balls and began shooting pool. Pete and I sat on the couch listening to soft jazz on the radio. Listening to the music made me think of Muriel again. I missed her and wished I could speak to her. I found some paper and a pen and sat down and wrote to her. I told her all about what I was doing, the training camp and sparring with Tony Canzoneri and that I missed her. I mailed it off the next morning.

We trained exceptionally hard the last week, and Tony was in the best shape he ever was and ready to meet Harry Dubinsky at Ebbets Field. We packed up and went back to the city. Saturday night we sat in our ringside seats waiting for the ten-round fight to begin.

Tony outpointed Dubinsky and won by a decision. We all converged into the dressing room and Tony's manager, Sammy Goldman, handed fifty dollars to Al for me. Al only gave me twenty-five. His skimming me was getting old. Soon I would outsmart him. He scheduled me to fight Lou

Camps in a six-round bout at the Saint Nickolas Arena next week. I was in great shape and ready to fight.

Whitey and Ray lifted the ropes and I entered the ring. Tony Canzoneri was ringside and gave me a wink and I winked back before the first round bell sounded.

I was in the best physical and mental shape ever and ready to fight Camps who fought twenty-one fights and was undefeated. Well, I gave Mr. Lou Camps a free boxing lesson in six rounds and all I charged him was one undefeated record. I was paid one hundred dollars. I couldn't even enjoy my win because I was totally pissed off. Al wouldn't tell me the purse for the fight. I had a bad taste in my mouth for Al that wouldn't go away.

That night I went back home to Coney Island and decided to take it easy for a while. I felt that in my career as a boxer, I was always taken advantage of and it made me furious. I made a commitment to myself that I won't ever let someone use me again. I was through playing the fool. Money was hard to come by and the fight game was filled with hungry fighters all looking for a big payday, but I paid my dues.

I wanted to make the money I deserved for the fights I fought. *I* went in the ring, not the managers. I proved myself as a fighter, people in the business knew who I was and my record spoke for itself. The business end of the boxing world screwed me time and time again. It was as important as winning a bout, trusting a manager to give me a fair deal.

Thinking about this problem emptied me out. I was drained. I thought of Muriel, her genuine sincerity. She really cared for me—me, Danny London the man, not the boxer. I remembered our time together though short, and longed for her smile and her warm touch. I wanted to drown in her deep blue eyes. I decided go to Brownsville, Brooklyn, in the morning and surprise her.

I woke early and it was the beginning of a clear bright day. I did my two-mile roadwork, went back to the house, cleaned up and put on my sport clothes. I ate a light breakfast before I left the house and walked slowly to the subway. I stopped at a flower stand and bought a bouquet of wild flowers. I got off the train at Brownsville Station and walked with my chest out and my chin up with the flowers leading the way. I heard a loud yelling from the rooftop of Muriel's house.

"Danny! Danny!"

Her loud voice was probably heard a block away.

"Wait! I'll be right down."

She was so surprised and happy to see me. She kissed and hugged me. I was really taken back, and all I managed to do was hold out the bouquet. She grabbed the flowers and she kissed and hugged me all over again.

"Danny, what a surprise. I thought about you a lot and missed you every day."

I was still bewildered from the kisses and hugs when she took my hand and led me into the building.

"I want you to meet my parents."

Like a robot, I followed Muriel into her apartment where her mother sat at a sewing machine. Muriel introduced me to her mother who responded with a warm smile. Her father, who was seated on the sofa, gave me a grumpy look, stood up and limply shook my hand.

Muriel's mother asked me if I would like to stay for dinner.

"Sure."

Muriel was so excited. In between helping her mom with supper, she asked me a million questions about everything I did for the past three weeks. We ate a spaghetti and meatball dinner that filled the room with delicious aromas. Muriel's father started the conversation and talked about the old time boxing fights and how great the boxers of his day were. I wasn't too interested in his conversation but out of respect I listened. Her father still had a grumpy mood about him, and I'm sure it was in the best interest of his daughter.

After supper I took Muriel to the movies and she led the way to the very back row of the balcony. She never once looked at the screen, she was all over me and we made love right there in that theater. Muriel held on to me long after the show. I felt loved and wanted. I had feelings I'd never felt before. I couldn't stop looking at her remembering the beauty of her body. My first lovemaking was so natural with Muriel. We were happy and in love.

We left the movie house without knowing even the title of the movie. We walked holding hands with her head resting on my shoulder. I stood in front of her apartment building never wanting to leave her but I knew I had to.

"This week I'll be training hard every day for my next fight and I won't be able to see you."

"I want to see you every day but I understand. Best of luck in the fight and I pray you won't get hurt. I'll be waiting for you."

We kissed good night and held each other tightly. She was my girl now. I waited for her to enter the building and I took the subway home.

The next morning I ran on the boardwalk and trained in Stillman's Gym. I was waiting for Al to get me a fight. I lost faith in him a long time ago. I knew he was cutting the purse every fight and now I'd clear the air. I barged into his office. All the lost purse money came out in uncontrollable anger.

"Al, I want out, I'm leaving you."

"What the hell is wrong with you? No one will take care of you like me. What's your beef?"

Al became as pissed as I was.

"You don't give me what's coming to me. You take too much of the purse. I'm going out on my own."

I walked out of Al's office and never looked back. He was still talking and yelling profanities, but I was through with him.

29

It was 1935. I was twenty-one years old and felt that the prime of my boxing career arrived. My relationship with Muriel grew and I was totally free from any contracts and managers. Managers and trainers were a dime a dozen and the best of the crop were with the best fighters. It was clear to me the managers housed many fighters in their stables and became rich overnight by skimming from the purses. The trainers worked hard getting the fighters in shape and they, like the boxers, struggled to survive.

I thought about my old friend Hymie Miller and wondered how he was doing. I decided to go and see him at the pool hall.

"Danny, it's great to see you, you look great. How have you been?"

Hymie made feel welcomed and I felt that he was truly concerned about me.

"I'm feeling fine and in good shape. Can I have a word with you?"

"Sure, let's go in my office."

"I left my manager, Al Weil, and I was wondering if you were still interested in managing me?"

"Are you serious? I love you. I'll take care of you and get you good fights. Why did you leave Al?"

"Al wasn't honest with me. He continually skimmed the purses and never shared what the payouts were."

"Things will be different with me, Danny. Don't worry. Stay in shape and I'll have fights for you soon."

Hymie Miller shook my hand and said that there would be no written contract between us and if there was ever a problem, about money or anything else, I should come to him. I felt that Hymie put everything out in the open and it made me feel that he truly had my best interest at heart.

Maybe this time someone will treat me fairly and I'll advance in the boxing arena and increase my prestige and pocketbook. Hymie paid for my workout time at Stillman's and Whitey and Ray still trained me.

Hymie was true to his word and scheduled a fight with Dominick Nico at Luna Park for Saturday night. I was amazed at how fast Hymie made things happen. My mind and body were in top-notch shape. I could hardly wait to fight again.

Whitey lifted the ropes and I entered the ring and started to loosen up by jabbing and moving around. I glanced in my opponent's corner and Nico looked back with a cold, hard stare. He definitely was trying to intimidate me, but it wasn't going to work. He was a well-built Italian with large forearms.

The referee called us into the center and gave us instructions. Heading back to my corner, I looked around the Luna Park Arena and it was packed with fans ready to see a good fight.

The bell rung and Nico charged me like a bull. I swiftly moved to the side and circled him. He couldn't put a glove on me and his frustration was rising. His punches were wild and he was telegraphing. I had his number. The first round ended and I hadn't even worked up a sweat.

In the second round, Nico made the fatal mistake of using the same strategy he used in the previous round. He came toward me and I hit him with a solid jab to his nose and a right cross to his chin. He went down and was out. The referee gave a ten count and I had a second-round knockout. The referee raised my hand high and announced me the winner.

Hymie came in the dressing room and handed me two hundred dollars and congratulated me on a superb fight.

"Danny, next Saturday night we'll be at Braddock Bowl in Fort Lee, New Jersey. I scheduled a ten-round bout with Al Todisco."

Things were changing for the better. I made the right decision to have Hymie manage me. I should have made this decision a long time ago. We were a team now and finally for the first time I knew my fighting career was on the upswing.

"After you clean up and dress I'm taking you, Whitey, and Ray to dinner."

We went to an upscale restaurant and celebrated the first win in our new partnership. I felt terrific. I went home, handed Mom some money, and she was happy and I was happy. I went to bed and slept soundly.

The next week passed quickly. I trained hard every day at Stillman's from morning till night. I was ready. I entered the Braddock Bowl dressing room with Whitey and Ray. Ray taped my hands while Whitey gave background on Al Todisco's boxing skills.

"Todisco's a boxer, not a slugger. He knows how to punch and his punches are powerful. He's a trained boxer who knows how to move around in the ring. Stay away from him, make him run after you and use your jab to slow him down. Don't get cocky. He's a professional, this is how he makes his living."

Whitey did his homework on the opponents and his advice was always on the money.

We left the dressing room and as I entered the ring, I saw that Todisco was already there moving around like a caged lion. The referee called us to the center of the ring and gave us our instructions. Todisco up close was as solid a fighter as I'd ever seen. His stomach muscles were ripped and his legs and arms were huge. His head was shaved clean and he was mean looking.

The first round bell rung and as I left the corner Whitey yelled, "Stay away from him! Box him!"

Todisco was a pugilist and the fight was even until the eighth round when I landed a right cross to Todisco's chin. The punch ended the match. The referee raised my arm in the air and the fans cheered for five minutes. They were pleased with the fight and outcome.

The advice Whitey gave me earlier, I used in this fight and every fight after.

The dressing room was filled with reporters and cops who wouldn't let any of my family or friends or Hymie come in. Finally, he made them understand that he was my manager and they let him pass. He made his way through the crowd and handed me two hundred dollars. Life was great.

"Danny, we're back in Luna Park in two weeks. I pulled some strings and got you a match with Al Ragone."

Whitey and Ray said that I needed to rest for a week and then start training for the Ragone fight. I followed their directions. They knew the rest would strengthen my body and mind.

A few days later Hymie called and told me to stop by his office that he wanted to talk to me. That afternoon I went to see him and he seemed troubled and preoccupied.

"I have to go to Los Angeles and take care of some pressing business. While I'm gone Julie Rosenstein and George Shepard will manage you."

Julie Rosenstein and George Shepard were tough strong-arm guys for one of the local unions. They were loyal friends to Hymie.

"Rosenstein and Shepard will be here in a few minutes and I'll introduce them to you and make sure they understand their role while I'm away is to take care of you. Get you fights and pay you fair."

A few minutes later, Julie Rosenstein knocked and entered with George Shepard.

"Danny, this is Julie Rosenstein and George Shepard. They'll take care of you while I'm in Los Angeles."

We shook hands and sat down and talked about the upcoming bout with Al Ragone at Luna Park. Hymie's facial expressions never changed throughout the meeting. His eyes were red with dark circles. It looked as though he hadn't slept in a week.

Hymie said good-bye and wished me luck.

"Danny, I'll stay in touch and if you need anything just ask Rosenstein."

I started to train for the Ragone fight and hoped Rosenstein and Shepard wouldn't screw me while Hymie was away.

I was on a roll. Ragone went down from a right cross in the sixth round. The referee raised my hand high in the air and I soaked in the roars from the crowd.

I was paid two hundred and felt a little more confident that my new managers, Rosenstein and Shepard, were going to follow Hymie's direction. Rosenstein was a big guy with a strong Brooklyn accent. He had a reputation for taking no s—— from anybody around the city. His buddy, Shepard, matched his size and strength. They looked like book ends. Rosenstein booked one fight after another.

"Danny, I've already scheduled a bout with Pat Robertson at the Lenox Club in Atlantic City in two weeks."

This was the break I waited for forever—terrific fights against legitimate boxers for decent money. I was in the best physical shape and my mental outlook was positive. I was blessed with honest managers and the best trainers. I was ready to take on the world.

At the beginning of the next week I was back on the boardwalk running and back in the gym sparring and working out. I was in great shape for the Robertson fight. Whitey and Ray praised me for my dedication to the intense training schedule.

There was a sold-out house Saturday night at the Lenox Club in Atlantic City. I saw many familiar faces. Guess what? I had a following. I didn't want to let my fans down, but more importantly I didn't want to let myself down. I was on a win streak and winning felt great.

I stood in my corner and eyed Pat Robertson as he eyed me. He was in excellent shape and so was I. The referee gave us our instructions as Robertson intensely stared in my eyes trying to make me afraid. That tactic never worked with me; the proof would be in the fight.

Robertson was a professional and I remembered Whitey's pearls of wisdom, respect the fighter and don't be cocky and box your fight. He wasn't a slugger, he was tactful and strategic but he only lasted until the sixth round. He was counted out.

Rosenstein placed two hundred dollars in my hand in the dressing room. He said that he and Shepard booked a main event bout with the undefeated Harry Jeffra in Baltimore's Carlins' Park. Jeffra was an extremely touted and highly ranked boxer and I was sure that Rosenstein pulled some strings using his strong union skills to get this fight. Whitey was serious.

"We have only three days to get you ready for Jeffra. You must concentrate on your speed, light on your feet, moving quickly around the ring using your most important asset, your ability to jab, jab, jab, nonstop, never letting up."

I trained following Whitey and Ray's routine of speed in the ring and jabbing. I was ready and they knew I was ready; my confidence level was at its peak. We packed the car and headed down to Baltimore. It was awhile since I was out of the city and the ride's scenery relaxed and refreshed my spirit. We checked into our hotel and then headed to the gym and I worked out for a couple of hours. Jeffra was in the gym, but he never looked my way. He continued with his workout program and I stayed focused on mine.

Saturday morning, Whitey didn't want me to work out or do road.

"I want you to save your energy for the fight. No junk food."

Friends and family were in attendance. There was standing room only. The stage was set and I was eager to get in the ring with a boxer of Jeffra's status.

Ray taped my hands and put gloves on me while Whitey chapped my ears with his redundant instructions.

"Stay away from Jeffra and use your deadly weapon, the jab. Jeffra's tough. Keep sharp. Time to get into the ring and put him away."

I was pumped as we walked to the ring. Whitey and Ray lifted the ropes and I climbed in. I looked into the crowd, Al Tesh and my brother, Jack, were sitting in front rows and next to Jack was Muriel throwing me kisses and yelling with her screechy voice. "Good luck, Danny!"

I was sure she convinced Jack to bring her.

Jeffra entered the ring and never looked at me. He was the favorite by the roar of the crowd, I was the underdog. The ring announcer introduced us and made it a point to let the crowd know that Jeffra was undefeated. We went center ring and listened to the referee's instructions. Jeffra never looked at me. We went back to our corners and waited for the bell.

The first round was even and I experienced the artistic work of the well-trained Harry Jeffra, but I was also aware that he realized quickly that I was someone to be reckoned with. In the second round, Jeffra became more aggressive and took a few of my jabs, which made him think twice about that strategy.

I won the third round by outpunching him and my strategy worked. He was impatient and frustrated. The fourth round was a wash. Jeffra made a big mistake in the fifth and walked in to a solid jab to his left eye and a right cross to the chin. He went down for a count of ten and never got up. The roof came down on Carlins' Park when the referee raised my hand.

"Winner by knockout, Danny London."

Whitey and Ray hoisted me up on their shoulders and carried me back to the dressing room with an entourage of people behind us. Somehow Muriel got to the dressing room and was waiting for me at the door. The guys put me down and she jumped in my arms and began kissing and hugging me.

"Congratulations, Danny. What a great fight."

"Thank you. You should have told me you were coming."

"I wanted to surprise you."

I carried her into the dressing room and the police and reporters pushed their way in. It was chaotic.

"I'll see you after I get dressed."

Muriel kissed me again and left the dressing room. Whitey ran over overwhelmed with excitement.

"Great fight and big win."

Rosenstein handed me three hundred dollars. The best payday to date.

"Great fight, Danny. Don't pack your bags. I arranged a deal for you to fight Joe Rivers in two weeks right here at Carlins' Park."

Joe Rivers was a Mexican who was on the rise in the featherweight division. I was anxious to fight him. His arms were huge and he was in tip-top shape. His knockout punch was his claim to fame. He moved rapidly from the lightweight class to the featherweight class.

We left the dressing room and Muriel, Jack, Al, and many Coney Island friends were waiting to greet me. I invited them back to my hotel for a celebration. We had a great time and Muriel wanted to know when I'd be back home.

"Not for a couple of weeks. I'm fighting Joe Rivers in two weeks, right here in Baltimore."

"Can I stay with you? Just kidding, I know you'll be training and I'd be a distraction, but a good distraction."

She giggled and I knew exactly what she meant.

"I miss you."

"After this next fight, I'll take some time off and we'll spend some time together."

"I'm so glad. Good luck with your next fight."

Muriel kissed me for a long time and when she finally finished, Jack and Al wished me luck and they left the room and headed back to New York. Rosenstein came over to me and said that he wanted to go over some things.

"Sit down, Romeo."

He chuckled over his little joke and got a big kick out of himself. He said that he paid up front for gym time so I could start training immediately and prepare for the River's fight. I couldn't wait to train. Before bed I thought of Muriel, my girlfriend. The word sounded strange but I liked it. I hoped she got home safely. I slept soundly and woke early the next morning and did a two-mile run. I returned to the hotel, ate a light breakfast, and went to the gym. Whitey, Ray, and Rosenstein were waiting for me to start the training routine for the Rivers' fight.

This schedule was grueling for the next couple of days, roadwork, workouts, and sparring partners in the ring. Wednesday before the fight, I felt unbeatable, in the best shape ever when a sparring mate hit me with two solid shots to the lower ribs on my left side. Sharp pain erupted and I knew he hurt me badly. I never said a word to Whitey and Rosenstein. I hoped it would heal by Saturday.

We entered the ring Saturday night with the ritual of introductions and referee's instructions. Rivers looked solid and in optimal shape. I was suffering in pain but didn't want the fight to be postponed. I fought injured. By the ninth round, my left eye was swollen and almost closed and my ribs were on fire with excruciating pain. The fight was stopped and Rivers won. Back at the dressing room, Whitey and Rosenstein wanted to know what the hell was wrong with me.

"You weren't punching and you looked like you were in pain. What was going on? You acted like you didn't want to be in the ring. Goddamn, tell us what the f——k just happened in there!"

I told them about my ribs and all hell broke loose. They screamed and ranted so loudly that I felt the entire arena heard them. They were so pissed off at me. Their profanities went on and on and on. I didn't think they'd ever shut up.

They were completely silent on the drive back to New York. I was grateful. They dropped me home and we parted on a sour note. A few days later, a powder keg exploded in my head and I packed my bags. I informed my parents that I was going to the coast, not to worry, I'd write to them. My curt attitude took them back and they never said a word. I kissed them and left. I went to the telegraph office and sent Hymie Miller a telegram informing him I was coming to Los Angeles. I took a taxi to Grand Central Station and bought my ticket.

30

It took the train three and a half days to get to Los Angeles Depot and when I arrived Hymie Miller was there to greet me. He carried my bags to his car and we headed for his home. On the way, I told him about my loss to Joe Rivers.

"Take it easy here until your ribs heal and when you're ready to train I'll line up fights in Los Angeles for you."

His home was cozy and comfortable. I had my own room. Hymie's Uncle Charlie lived with him and he did all the cooking. He was one hell of a chef. I relaxed and went to the beach. I walked the beach and swam in the ocean and became stronger each day.

The next week I started training at the Main Street Gym. My ribs were better so I began training harder. I didn't have a trainer but I used my training experience to help me get in shape. I worked out for the next two weeks and a trainer at the gym started to match me with sparring mates. This really helped my workouts.

Uncle Charlie prepared decadent meals and we ate together every evening.

"Danny, I set up a fight with Herbie Hansford at the Hollywood Legion Arena this Saturday night."

"I'm ready. My ribs are healed and I've trained hard."

Hymie and Uncle Charlie drove me to the arena.

"Danny, before we go into the dressing room, I want to introduce you to some people I'd like you to meet."

Hymie took me into an area with cushioned seats and introduced me to Mae West, Clark Gable, Bing Crosby, William Powell, Al Jolson, Eddie Cantor, and Tom Mix. They were huge fight fans and eager to see me fight. We shook hands and they wished me the best of luck. The arena was packed and I was ready for the bout.

In the dressing room while a trainer taped my hands, I turned to Hymie.

"How do you know all the movie stars?"

"I'm well connected in this town and have a lot of business dealings with many celebrities and political people."

I was impressed with Hymie. He was well connected yet for the most part I only knew he had a delicatessen that was popular throughout the city.

We left the dressing room and I entered the ring and went to my corner. For the first time, I laid eyes on Herbie Hansford. He was big shouldered and in terrific shape. The normal fanfare of introductions and instructions began. When Hansford was introduced, the crowd erupted; when I was introduced, you could hear a pin drop. It was apparent that he was the local favorite and I was the unknown.

The first round bell rung and we were on our feet in the middle of the ring. I heard the voice of Doc, "Jab, jab, jab, Danny."

Hansford came face to face and threw stiff powerful jabs that never touched me. I knew his number by the fourth round. His fighting strategy became predictable. I threw two straight jabs to his chin and a right cross that landed on his right cheekbone. He was out cold.

A memorable experience resurfaced when the referee held my hand high in the air. The crowd was dumbfounded at first. They didn't know what to make of this newcomer, then they came alive with applause and cheers. In the dressing room Hymie handed me four hundred dollars.

"You certainly fooled the crowd. Handsford was their favorite boy and you took him out. What a fantastic upset! I've signed you to fight his brother, George Hansford, who wants revenge for Herbie."

The fight was scheduled at the same venue in two weeks. I took it easy for the next few days. I went to the beach, walked around Hollywood, and took in the sights of downtown Los Angeles to pass the time. I was down on Vine Street walking and window shopping when George Raft and his bodyguard, Mac Grey, approached me.

"Do you think you can win against George Hansford?"

"Well, I don't know but I'll give him the best fight I can."

"We'll be rooting for you, best of luck."

I thanked George Raft and he and this bodyguard walked away. I bought a copy of the *Los Angeles Times* and started reading a story about Mae West betting five hundred dollars on George Hansford to win the fight. She made a wrong decision. I knew I was in great shape and training hard, so he'd have a worthy opponent.

I entered the ring on Saturday night and saw George Hansford sitting in his corner. Wow, he looked like his brother, Herbie. Their physiques were identical; they looked like twins. I hoped they fought the same as well. The only difference in the ring this time is when the announcer gave the introductions, the crowd cheered louder for me. When the bell rung, George headed straight toward me. He was much more aggressive than his brother and he was more skilled with his punches, but his talent was not enough. He made it only one round further than Herbie. I dropped him face down in the fifth. The bell saved him, I won by decision. What an upset! Back in the dressing room Hymie filled my hand with five hundred dollars.

"Congrats, Danny, what an upset. We'll be fighting Ray Campo here in two weeks."

I took it easy for a couple of days. I walked down Hollywood Boulevard, and ran into an old friend of mine from Brooklyn, Mickey Phillips. He worked for the actor Ray Milland.

"Danny, I wasn't in town to see the fights but congratulations on two great wins."

"Thanks, Mickey."

Mickey and I talked and caught each other up on Brooklyn's local news.

"Danny, how would you like to come to Paramount Studio with me?"

"I'd love to. I have nothing to do today."

Mickey's car was parked nearby. It was a sporty convertible with the top down. The sky was bright blue and the air was fresh. It felt great and this was a needed distraction from my normal day at a sweat-soaked gym. Mickey pulled up to the gate, showed his ID, and the security guard motioned us in. I was amazed at the enormous size of the studio's property. Mickey parked in his reserved spot. I guess he was doing pretty well for himself. We entered a building filled with movie equipment and building materials. I followed

Mickey to a cafeteria where a host of actors were eating breakfast, talking and laughing.

"Good morning, everyone. This is my old friend from Brooklyn, New York, the classiest boxer in the fight game, Mr. Danny London."

My eyes lit up when I saw Bing Crosby, Clark Gable, Gary Cooper, William Frawley, and Ben Blue, some of the most famous actors in the world. They stood up and applauded. I was stunned. Clark Gable walked over and put his hands up in a boxing jester and began sparring with me. Everyone got a kick out of it and started laughing and cheering. They invited me to join them for breakfast and I sat and we talked. Some saw the fight against Herbie Hansford and commented on how I outboxed him and won a great fight. We talked until one by one they had to leave to be on set. I spent the rest of the day watching a movie being made. I invited Mickey back to Hymie's house and he accepted.

When we entered Hymie's house the aroma of savory food filled our nostrils. Hymie greeted us and I introduced him to Mickey. Excitedly, I told Hymie about my day at Paramount Studios and the warm greeting I received from the great stars. We shared a sumptuous meal and had an enjoyable evening talking with each other. Mickey assured me that he'd be ringside for the Campo fight. I gave him two tickets and he said that he'd bring his boss, Ray Milland.

Hymie was sitting in the living when I returned. He said that he needed to talk with me.

"Danny, it seems as though after the George Hansford win, every boxer in the area wants a piece of you. I think you're going to be busy for the next three months. Already, I scheduled four fights, Deal Barnes, Mark Diaz, Pete

De Grasso, and Varias Milling. All of the fights are two weeks apart."

My mind raced. Without a moment to lose, I started to get ready for the fights. It was an extremely hectic and demanding schedule forcing me to stay focused and in shape.

"Great, Hymie. I'll be ready. Thanks."

"That's what I want to hear. I'm here for you. Keep winning and the money and fights will keep coming."

31

I was up early the next morning doing roadwork and I headed to the gym after. I never let up on the training and I pushed myself harder than ever. My trainer was glad I worked hard never once complaining, and he complimented me my seriousness. I was never cocky or complacent. I left after a great workout and headed back to Hymie's house. A man on the street approached me.

"I'm a good friend of Julie Rosenstein, your manager, and I'm here to bring you back to New York."

"I'm not going anywhere with you. Rosenstein is not my manager. Hymie Miller is my manager. What are you going to do about that?"

The guy was stuck for words and looked stupid. He was a thug, hired by Rosenstein to scare me. Probably, Rosenstein gave this mope money for train fare and the zoot suit he was wearing and told him that he was to bring me back. I left him standing on the corner and went to Hymie's.

Hymie's was in the living room reading the paper when I entered. I told him all about the ridiculous thug and how Rosenstein was trying to pull a fast one. Hymie jumped to his feet and went nuts, yelling like a mad man in an insane asylum. He ran out signaling me to follow. We took off in his car and sped down the road. He drove like a maniac and I flew all over the front seat. He screeched his brakes and leaned on the horn until a guy ran from a house and jumped in the car. Hymie slammed the car in gear and floored the gas. He never let up till we reached the gym. The idiot was still there, standing outside. Hymie and the guy ran over to him.

"You son of a b——h! Rosenstein sent you to f——k with Danny and me?"

Hymie knew the guy who looked small and embarrassed right now. Hymie got him in a headlock, dragged him into the alley and started whaling on him unmercifully. He was cut and bleeding from every part of his head. Hymie's friend didn't do anything. We just watched the guy get pummeled. He lay in the alley with his new zoot suit covered in blood.

"Get the f——k out of town and tell Rosenstein to go to hell."

Hymie and I never spoke about the incident. I was resting for a few days before the Ray Campo fight when Hymie took me and a couple of his friends to the Hal Roach Studios.

Clark Gable was making a new movie, *San Francisco*. The director asked if we wanted to be in the movie, he had small walk-on parts. Even better, we'd get paid. We agreed, but it wasn't as easy as I thought.

It was eight hours repeating the same thing. I was bored to death. I found out after a grueling day that it was impossible to please a director.

I found a hiding place and took a nap. When I finally woke up, the walk-ons were not needed any more. The director was confused when he saw me.

"Where did you go? You missed most of the movie."

"I was taking a nap, I was so bored."

Everyone laughed and he gave everyone fifteen dollars, even me. We went back to Hymie's and Uncle Charlie was waiting with dinner.

Saturday night, I was in the ring ready for Ray Campo. There were many familiar faces in the crowd, friends and Hollywood stars. The bell rung and Campo came out fast and I immediately put the brakes on him with my left jab. He lasted four rounds. The referee raised my hand high in the air, winner by knockout.

As usual Hymie rewarded me well. The next fights against Deal Barnes, Mark Diaz, Pete De Grasso, and Varias Milling were all wins and the money flowed into my pocket. My reputation around Southern California grew and I became recognized and popular in the arena. I felt like a star.

After dinner one evening with Hymie and Uncle Charlie I went for a walk down Vine Street and Hollywood Boulevard. I met face to face with Frankie Darro, a well-known star.

"Danny London, I've attended all your bouts, you're a great boxer. Will you teach me how to box?"

"Training to box takes time. Aren't you too busy making movies?"

"You're right, I don't have much time on my hands. Do you like wrestling?"

"It doesn't interest me, I never watch it."

"Why don't you come with me to the Legion tonight? We can watch some wrestling matches."

I went with Frankie Darro to the Hollywood Legion and we were given free admission. I was so bored that I fell asleep and Frankie had to shake my shoulder to wake me up. I couldn't understand why wrestling was so entertaining to him. We left the Legion and went to a local coffee shop for a cup of coffee and piece of cake. Our conversation was all about boxing until it was interrupted when the customers recognized Frankie. He had to stop talking and sign autographs. I got home late that night and found Hymie was waiting up for me.

"I was worried about you. It's late. Is everything okay?"

I told him about Frankie Darro and he was relieved. He was glad that I had a good time and laughed when I told him about the wrestling.

The next morning, Hymie woke me and told me to get my things together.

"We're driving back to New York."

I didn't ask why because he sounded serious and in a hurry. He offered no explanations. It was as if he was on a military mission with no time to lose and wouldn't divulge why it was so important to get back to New York. He gave Uncle Charley orders to take care of the house and that he would be in touch.

The long drive cross country gave me time to think about my future, my future in boxing. Would I get a chance at the title? I also thought about Muriel. I wondered if she still cared about me. I wasn't a thoughtful boyfriend. I just left for three months and never said a word to her. Maybe she had a new boy friend now and I had no right to blame her.

It took us three and a half days to get to New York and when we arrived Hymie drove directly to his mother's house in Coney Island.

"Danny, you can stay here for as long as you like."

I decided to stay away from my parents for a while. Hymie's mother was accommodating, giving me a clean room. I got myself situated and a couple days later I went to visit my parents.

I walked in around suppertime. I knew the family would be together and eating supper and I'd have an opportunity to see them all. Everyone was happy to see me. They hugged and kissed me. My mother's eyes welled up as she hugged and kissed me and to my surprise my father greeted me the same. I gave my mother two hundred dollars and she let out a little scream.

"Where are you staying?"

"At Hymie Miller's mother's house for a while."

The look on my parent's faces indicated that they didn't like the idea. I explained that I needed peace and quiet for now and hoped they'd understand. I enjoyed a wonderful dinner with the family and we talked about how their life was hard and they needed money.

"Don't worry about money."

Mom got up and hugged me. I felt the love and support of my family and I realized how much they needed my love and support.

The next day I visited some old friends in Coney Island. They were all glad I was home. They shook my hand and congratulated me on my impressive wins on the West Coast. I spent the entire day with them. I slept well that night. I needed my rest for the next day.

I planned to go and see Muriel. I needed to know if I still had a chance with her. I hoped so.

32

The next day I took the subway to Brownsville and the ride went too fast, I didn't know if I was ready to face Muriel. I got off the train and slowly walked to her building. I wore my best sports clothes and stopped for a beautiful bouquet of flowers hoping they would let Muriel know I really do care. I knocked on her apartment door and Muriel answered. She was so surprised. Her screeching voice was probably heard throughout the building.

"Danny, Danny, you're back. You're home. You look so good. You have a beautiful California tan."

Muriel jumped on me hugging me tightly and kissing every inch of my face passionately. She loved and missed me. Her parents welcomed me and her father actually treated me with respect. I stayed for dinner and as we ate I told them about my many fights in Los Angeles and the many movie stars I met. They couldn't believe it.

After dinner, Muriel and I went out for a long walk. We went to the park, sat on a bench, and talked and talked about our feelings for each other. For the first time I felt like I really got to know her and I loved what I learned. As she spoke I was swallowed up in her deep blue eyes. She was truly a beautiful young woman and I finally noticed it.

"Danny, I love you and I want to marry you as soon as possible."

Without hesitation I answered her. "Muriel, I love you too, but we need to plan and be patient. I still have to train and make more money. I might have a shot for the title."

"I understand, you're a professional boxer and it's been hard for you. I understand and I'll wait for you, even though I don't want to. I long to be with you."

We stayed on the bench in the park for a long time hugging and kissing. We would be true to each other and I would see her every free moment I had.

Hymie booked me a couple of fights around New York and out of town. I won and lost, it was a struggle to get a good fight and the money fights were scarce.

It was 1937 and I had a ray of hope when Harry Jeffra became featherweight champion. He took the title from Sixto Escobar. I was happy for Jeffra, he was a skilled boxer. This would be my chance to get the title fight. I knew I could knock Jeffra out again. I wanted Hymie to make this happen, but Hymie said that Jeffra's manager was keeping him away from me because I knocked his lights out the last time.

When Hymie told me the news about the manager's decision I became irate and annoyed with Hymie for not making it happen with his many connections. I was sure he could have made this happen.

"Danny, I'm going back to Los Angeles to open a larger delicatessen and while I'm gone Irving Cohen will be taking care of you."

I didn't know how to take this news from Hymie but what could I do? He was always fair with me so I believed he had to do this and I went along with his decision.

Irving Cohen was an okay guy and I got along with him. He got me a couple of fights around New York and I won a couple and lost a couple by bad decisions from the judges.

I received a telegram and a ticket from Hymie to return to the coast. He notified Irving Cohen, they communicated on a regular basis. This time I let everyone know I was leaving. My parents and siblings were sad but they understood. My biggest dilemma was telling Muriel that I had to go back out to the coast. I took her out to dinner and prayed she'd understand why I had to leave.

"How long will you be gone?"

"Hymie has scheduled some excellent fights and if things work out for me, maybe I'll get a shot at the title."

"I love you and I'll wait for you. I'll never get in the way of your dream."

We kissed and hugged. She was great. She didn't make me feel bad. I really loved her and her understanding made me love her more. Early the next morning I was in Grand Central Station waiting to board the train west. I wondered why everything with Hymie was mysterious and spontaneous. The train left the station and I was anxious to get there. The ride seemed faster than my previous trips, and before I knew it I was in Los Angeles with Hymie waving to me. Hymie put his arm around my shoulder and squeezed.

"Do you have fights lined up?"

"Yes, you'll rest for a week and then we'll get back to work."

We loaded my luggage in the car and drove to his new delicatessen in Hollywood.

The day was a normal Los Angeles day, warm and clear. Hymie pulled in front of the deli.

"Danny, close your eyes until I tell you to open them."

I figured Hymie wanted to surprise me with the beautiful renovations in the deli. I held his arm while he led me in. The aromas of Jewish delicacies filled my nose.

"Okay, open your eyes."

Oh my God, standing in front of me was Mutty. I was shocked. He bear hugged me.

"Why didn't you tell me you were coming out to the coast?"

"We wanted to surprise you and Hymie invited me to come out to the coast and help him in the new deli and I jumped at the chance, so I could support you in the boxing matches. I missed my old friend."

We sat down at a table and a beautiful waitress came over and took our order. We sat and talked while we ate lunch. We talked about the old days in Brooklyn and our trip across country in the freight trains. Hymie told us how the movie stars made his deli famous by making it their favorite place to eat and their favorite place to order food to be delivered to the movie sets. It was good to be here with these guys, my best friends. By this time, I was knocked out from the long trip and the excitement.

We said our good-byes to Mutty and I told him I'd catch up to him later. We drove to Hymie's new house. It was more beautiful and much bigger than the other house and filled with elegant furnishings. The only remnant from the old house was Uncle Charlie. He was here cooking and taking care of the house. Hymie led me to my room and

I unpacked. I was exhausted. I sat on the bed, fell back, and slept. The next morning, I woke up late. I took a hot shower, shaved, dressed, and walked down to Hymie's deli. I met Hymie and Mutty and we enjoyed breakfast together. I had a copy of the *Los Angeles Times* and I opened it to the sports section where there was a story about Harry Jeffra, the featherweight champ.

"Hymie, Jeffra's the champ. Can you get me a fight with him now?"

"I got a call from a guy in Baltimore that said if you throw the fight with Jeffra, he'll pay you five thousand dollars."

I couldn't taste my food. It was stuck in my throat. I couldn't believe what Hymie just said. He was present when I knocked Jeffra out. I was mad and insulted. Why did he want me to take a dive? My entire outlook on boxing was losing its flair, and of everyone I knew, I couldn't believe Hymie would suggest this, my manager.

"F——k no! I'd never take a dive! Tell those assholes I'm a legit boxer and I want a legit shot at the title with the champ."

Mutty and Hymie were wide eyed. They never saw me unleash fury like this before. I pushed the plate of food off the table and left the deli. A few days later I decided to get back in the gym and start training and get ready for my fight with Tony Chavez in the Olympic Arena in Los Angeles. The fight was three weeks away and my attitude was sour and at an all-time low. I had to focus on this ten-round bout. Chavez was a tough man with a good record.

Hymie was keeping his distance from me, and I was not going to let what happened go away too easy. My trainer worked hard with me to get me in shape. He did his homework on Chavez. Saturday night arrived and

Hymie, Mutty, and the trainer drove me to the Olympic Arena. There wasn't any conversation on the way. I sat in the dressing room while the trainer taped my hands and put the gloves on me. I was in fine shape and ready for the fight. We made our way to the ring and I sat on my stool while the trainer gave me some last-minute instructions.

"You're one of the best featherweights in the business. Move around in the ring and stay away from him. Let him do the chasing. Wait for the chance to use your deadly weapon and knock his lights out."

Every seat in the arena was filled. Even the fans in the standing room areas were shoulder to shoulder. Chavez had a huge Hispanic following and again I was the underdog. The ring announcer introduced us and the crowd roared. They were salivating for action. We went center ring and the referee gave us instructions.

The first round bell rung out, and Chavez came at me firing punches one after another for the entire three minutes of the round. Some of his wild punches landed everywhere on my body. His only purpose was to knock me out. He continued fighting this way throughout the fight. He probably threw a million punches, never stopping for a second in the three-minute rounds. My only defense was to use my jab. He gave me a couple low blows and the blind referee never warned him or called him on it. My eyes were swollen and almost closed, and the knuckle on my left hand was swollen and hurting. He injured me bit by bit, round by round. I couldn't get close to him to land a punch. I was pummeled with punches that took their toll on my body. I lost to Chavez in a ten-round decision. Chavez fought an excellent fight and won. I admired his skill in the ring. I shook his hand and congratulated him on a good fight.

"Sorry about the low blows, the ref should have called me on it."

I just nodded and walked away. Hymie walked in the dressing room and never uttered a word to me. Pain shot through every part of my body, I was hurting too badly to confront Hymie about the purse. Tonight, I lost the fight and a friend. I went to a Turkish bath and stayed all night.

33

In the morning, my body was sore but not hurting. I felt a little better. I needed a friend, someone to talk with and feel good about myself again. I thought about Muriel. I guess I was lovesick for her. I needed to see her, be close to her. I walked into Hymie's deli and he was at the counter. Lo and behold, he decided to speak to me.

"How do you feel?"

"I'm sore and my left knuckle's hurt. I'm going back to New York, I'll be back Christmas."

Hymie's face reddened and he started to shake. It was clear he didn't want to hear what I said.

"Is this Jeffra thing still bothering you? You need to let it go, forget about it and move on."

"I gotta do what I gotta do."

"Okay, you're the boss and free to do what you want."

He reached into his pocket and handed me three hundred dollars. Was he kidding? For a ten-round bout, I was sure I should have made more. Let the Jeffra thing go, forget it. *No*, he knows he was wrong. He should have made the fight for the championship happen. I'll never forget it!

"Solly Kreiger, who I managed for awhile, is heading back to New York, if you want you can travel with him. He was the middleweight champ."

"I'll go with him."

At noon, Solly picked me up at Hymie's house and I threw my stuff in his car and we left.

"Hymie gave me three hundred dollars for the ten rounder against Chavez."

"Danny, Hymie pulled the same crap on me, that's why I'm going back to New York. Our partnership changed, he wasn't honest and I won't stand for that s——t."

My relationship with Hymie changed too. My history with managers was consistent. I always wound up on the short end of the stick.

Solly and I talked about boxing, fighters, managers, trainers, and our wins and losses over the years. He was still a young man, but he wanted out of the fight game all together. He wanted a normal day job that would support his lifestyle. It took us four days to get to New York. Solly dropped me off at my parent's house, and I thanked him and shook his hand. I enjoyed his company. He was an okay guy.

Every time I returned home I was welcomed with opened arms. I talked with my parents about my Los Angeles fights and they listened with interest. They asked about Mutty and Hymie and I said that they were fine.

I took time off to let my hand heal. I needed to see Muriel and see how she was doing. The next day I went to see her. She was overjoyed, the kisses kept on coming. We went to the park and sat on our favorite bench where Muriel opened up like a floodgate. She expressed how terribly unhappy she is with her parents.

"My parents are moving to Eastern Parkway near Utica Avenue. I don't want to live with them anymore. I can't stand it. I want to get married."

"Can you have a little more patience? We'll be married soon."

When Muriel's parents moved, they invited me to come live with them in their new apartment. I think they thought they were going to lose their daughter and this was their solution to keep her close. The building was modern with two elevators. Muriel's father was a manager at a fish market and he got me a job there. At this time, there wasn't any opportunity for fights in New York. I was bored and disgusted, and the job was an opportunity for me to fill my time and make money.

One Sunday afternoon Muriel, her Aunt Ruthie, and I took a walk on Eastern Parkway and stopped at a small park. Aunt Ruthie was known to be outspoken and I learned this firsthand.

"Why aren't you and Muriel married? Maybe she'll be your rabbit's foot and bring you luck."

Muriel was always honest and innocent with me on her feelings, but today I was pretty sure that she set me up and staged the walk with Aunt Ruthie so she could corral me. Aunt Ruthie's comment stayed with me all day. Maybe Muriel was the luck I needed to fulfill my dream. Marrying her was what I wanted to do, what was I waiting for? The next morning I gently nudged Muriel and took her hand in mine. I looked at her. She was snuggled under the blanket with only her tasseled hair and hypnotizing baby blues showing. I bent over, touched her cheek, and softly kissed her lips. Her eyes were glittering with questions.

"Get dressed."

"Where're we going?"

"Trust me and hold my hand."

We left the building tightly holding hands and walked around the corner to the jewelry store. Muriel never made a sound while I purchased a small gold ring and placed it on her finger. It fit perfect. I bent down on one knee and with her hand still in mine and asked her to marry me. I waited for her answer expecting one of her high-pitched screeches, but she tenderly placed her hands around my face and pulled me close.

"I love you with all my heart."

We practically ran to the municipal building and purchased a marriage license for two dollars. Muriel was blissful. She looked at the ring over and over and was pleased with my selection. Even though it was an inexpensive ring, it was worth a million dollars to her. The thin, simple circle of gold was as beautiful as our love. We were on cloud nine. Laughing, she kept pinching herself and me to make sure we weren't dreaming.

We went back to the apartment and shared our elation and license with her parents. Mouths gaping they stood and stared blankly at the two of us. They were shocked. After a few moments in a heated flurry of words, they wanted to know why they weren't informed earlier about our plans. Frankly, I didn't think I had to include them in my surprise. After we talked and explained the events leading up to getting the license, they were thrilled and wanted to plan a celebration. Muriel's mom went right to work, making a list of friends and relatives to invite. She called my mom and told her to make her list of friends and relatives and the invitations went out. At first, my parents, like Muriel's, were not thrilled. They thought they should've been told about our plans too. It was our wedding. We were the only people who needed prior notice.

The wedding was scheduled on a Sunday. We were waiting at the temple on Eastern Parkway for my parents. Everyone else who was invited arrived on time. They finally arrived late and looked mad and unhappy. It was obvious they didn't want me to get married, but they couldn't stop it now. They would get over it and I didn't care. I was a man and I made my own decisions.

We were married by twin Canters and I was pleased with the ceremony. It was brief and to the point. Apparently, it was extremely emotional to others for the synagogue was filled with weeping. I hoped the tears were joyous. Everyone who attended the ceremony came to our reception. The food and drinks flowed all night. The gifts were small yet generous. People gave from their hearts in hard times. We were touched and happy. Monday morning, I received a telegram.

> Fight against Jimmy Lancaster at Madison Square Garden, Friday night. Irving Cohen

Muriel broke down laughing. "I guess the honeymoon is postponed now."

Coyly she smiled and said that we would have plenty of time for a honeymoon after the fight, a lifetime.

I thought of Aunt Ruthie and her words that my luck might change if I married Muriel. I lost a honeymoon, but had a fight. I guess it's all in your outlook.

The training the week before the fight was intense. Muriel waited for me each night and we ate dinner together. I felt ready for the fight and needed a good payday. Late Friday afternoon I went to the Boxing Commission to weigh in.

I weighed in but my opponent, Jimmy Lancaster, never showed up. The chickens——t son of a b——h disappeared.

"Irving, what the hell's going on here?'

"The Boxing Commission suspended Lancaster for not showing up to the weigh in."

"What the hell! I got married on Sunday and then had to postpone my honeymoon for this fight."

"I'm sorry. I had no idea, believe me."

I walked away from Irving and went home carrying a large chip on my shoulder. I was livid. I told Muriel the entire miserable story. I was finished with boxing, no more letdowns.

"I think I'll quit boxing and find a job."

I went out every day in the work world looking for a job. There was nothing out there for me. The reality of my life's situation sunk in. I devoted my life to boxing. I trained hard, stayed in perfect shape, and learned the skills. The harsh truth is I have no other skills or experiences other than boxing. My resume was short, a dishwasher or cleaning man. This reality was tough to face. Finally, Muriel's Uncle Robbie got us jobs in a factory. Muriel was operating a sewing machine and I was folding shoulder pads for ladies' dresses. The pay was twelve dollars a week. I felt humiliated and depressed and only lasted a couple of weeks before I knew I didn't belong there. I couldn't fold one more shoulder pad. My mind and heart were in the ring. I quit, went home, and waited for Muriel. I was afraid to tell her I quit. I couldn't work there any longer, it was demeaning and I felt less than a man. When Muriel came home, I sat her down and explained to her my dilemma of not being satisfied with the pay of a factory worker and that

Danny London

I was only meant to be a boxer. I am a boxer and I had to return to the ring.

"You've devoted most of your life training to be a champion and in my eyes you are. Go back in the ring where you belong. I'll stand by your side through the wins and the losses. I love you."

Muriel wrapped her arms around me and held me tight. She never said another word. She was a strong woman who made me know we were in this together, win or lose. I gathered all my boxing equipment, sat down with my father-in-law, and told him how things were going to be. As I talked, he sternly stared through me, but I kept going over my boxing plans and by the end of my talk, he was looking at me, smiling, and I knew that he understood.

"You're a world class boxer and still in your prime. You must follow your dream, no regrets, win or lose. I know you think because you married my daughter I should have a say in what you do in your life, but that's your business now. You're a man and if there's anything you need from me, ask. I'm here for you."

I was a little bewildered by his reaction. In the beginning of our relationship, he was skeptical, now he was supporting me and offering to help. I felt a strong bond. I was a part of the family.

"Pop, there is something you can do for me. Call my manager, Irving Cohen, and tell him I'm coming down to the gym to start training." My father-in-law called and sounded like a professional PR man. The ball was rolling in my corner.

When I arrived at Stillman's Gym, Whitey greeted me with open arms.

"Danny, we missed you. Welcome back."

Irving Cohen showed up and told me he scheduled a fight with Johnny Pena in two weeks at the Broadway Arena.

"We got work to do, Danny. We have to change the factory muscles to boxing muscles. Welcome back to life."

I trained hard for the next two weeks and Muriel stood by my side with love and support. I needed her to help me stay focused. She never once nagged me about not giving her any time. She was absolutely positive every day, no negative words and no distractions. We were fulfilling our dream of possibly one day I'd become the champ. We were doing it together.

Johnny Pena was on a winning streak, and Whitey drilled into my head how important this fight was for me. I was ready for the battle. My mind and body were in tune. Whitey trained me beyond the limits increasing every workout skill. Saturday night in the Broadway Arena dressing room Irving chatted in my ear. Whitey and Ray prepared me with last minute instructions. Whitey taped my hands and put my gloves on. Muriel came in, kissed me for luck, and quickly went to her ringside seat. Her entire family was in attendance along with mine. It was a sold-out arena and the crowd's intensity was building.

The crowd roared when I walked to the ring. I entered the ring and the crowd erupted with deafening screams. Johnny Pena was already in his corner staring me down. He looked fit and ready to take me down. The announcer made our introductions and our records enticed the crowd to erupt again. We received instructions from the referee and Pena looked magnified close up; he was ripped. We touched gloves and returned to our corners. The first round bell sounded and we moved to the center of the ring. For some reason, Al Peters popped in my head. His style of fighting was to keep his eyes on his opponent's gloves. Carefully I watched Pena's gloves and he started to telegraph his punches. I used my jab the entire round and they did their unnoticeable damage.

The rounds continued pretty much with the same pattern, but by the time the fifth round bell sounded, you could see that my constant jabs did considerable damage. Pena was badly hurt and the referee stopped the fight. I won by TKO.

I shook Pena's hand and graciously he said that I was a great boxer. The crowd roared. They were pleased and entertained with the outcome. The dressing room was filled with reporters and police. Muriel came in and kissed me.

"Great fight, see you at home."

Cohen slipped eight one hundred dollar bills into my hand. As always I wasn't satisfied. Whitey and Ray were hooting and hollering in the room saying it was a great fight and they were glad I was back. Irving took me home, and Muriel and her parents were waiting up for me. Her father jumped up when I went in the door.

"Great fight, Danny. You're definitely the best in your class."

We hugged and jumped around the living room laughing. Tonight, we were close. Muriel and I retired to our bedroom where I gave her the eight one hundred-dollar bills. She grinned so broadly that I thought her cheeks would explode. We got in bed and slept soundly in each other's arms.

The next day Hymie Miller called and congratulated me on a great win. He wanted me to return to the coast. He assured me that he'd book more fights and get me some small parts in movies.

"Danny, you can stay with me, like the old days. I have plenty of room for you and your wife."

I told Muriel about Hymie's call and invitation.

"Things are good for you here. Irving has more fights lined up for you and you are making the money. The money is coming in for you."

Muriel was right. I had to think seriously about what I was going to do. The next morning I decided to take a couple of days and clear my head. I picked up a paper to see the write-up on the Pena fight and headed back to the apartment to have a light breakfast with Muriel. As I ate, I flipped through the first few pages. A headline hit me right between the eyes.

Café Owner Shot in Bed by a Mysterious Intruder

HOLLYWOOD, CALIFORNIA Nov. 15—A man fired four shots at close range into Hymie Miller, 31. He was a movie actor, sports figure, and Hollywood café owner. Miller was recently cast in the movie *Robin Hood* and played many other minor roles. Also, Miller managed the boxer Danny London, out of New York. London came to California five years ago, fought many bouts in Hollywood, and was extremely successful. Miller was discovered critically wounded in his bed early this morning. His nose was shot off, his left hand was shot through, a bullet pierced his neck, and a bullet pierced through his left thigh and went through his right thigh. From his hospital bed, Miller described the brutal attack. "I heard a noise in the room and woke up and saw a man standing in the darkness. Before I could rise, the intruder started firing."

The gun was so close to Miller that he was marked with powder burns. Miller was unable to describe the gunman and knew of no one who wanted to harm him. He was scheduled to leave for work at Warner Brothers Studio this morning. Miller stayed conscious for eleven hours, then took a turn for the worse and died.

Why would anyone want to hurt Hymie? I tried to call his brother, Murry, but no one answered the phone. I thought that most likely Murry and his mother were already on a plane to Los Angeles. I thought to myself, What if I was sleeping in that room? I would've been shot.

I felt terrible about Hymie. We had our ups and downs but he was a good guy. He never deserved to be killed. I went back out and bought the *Los Angeles Times* to get more information about the senseless murder. They listed the stars in attendance at his funeral. Milton Berle, Irving Berlin, Al Jolson, the list went on. The headline on this article confused me.

Hymie Miller Knew Too Much

What did this mean? It was a mystery to everyone, a murder mystery.

I finally reached Hymie's mother and expressed my condolences. We talked for a while. I felt so sad for her. She was depressed over the untimely death of her son who was taken from her by violence. She was trying to manage the deli but it was hard. She asked if I'd ever consider coming back to the coast.

34

It was 1938 and I was married for about a year. I was boxing, winning and losing, back and forth. The fights were slowing down and I was getting older. Money was still hard to come by and Muriel and I were just getting by. I began thinking of Hollywood and maybe I could find work there through old friends. I sat down with Muriel and told her that we had to make plans for a better future with more opportunities.

"Muriel, I think I can find work as a prop man in the Hollywood studios. If I get a decent job there, then I'll send for you and we'll start over out west."

Muriel was all for it. She knew that there was nothing happening for us in New York. She said that she would stay with her parents until I sent for her.

I arrived in Los Angeles and took a taxi to Hymie's deli in Hollywood. When I walked in, Mrs. Miller went into hysterics. She ran over to me, threw her arms around me, and squeezed until I couldn't breathe. Finally, when she let go, she started to cry repeating Hymie's name over and over. It was sad and emotional.

"Danny, stay with me at Hymie's house, there's plenty of room. I'd appreciate the company. If you need work, you're welcome to help out in the deli."

The delicatessen was empty. A gloomy atmosphere prevailed throughout. Once the deli was filled with laughter and customers. No one came around since Hymie's death.

"Mrs. Miller, I'll help if you need me."

It didn't appear like any help was needed. There weren't any customers or outside orders from the studios. I had to find a job in Hollywood that paid well. There was nothing in New York and I had a few connections here. Maybe one of them would help me find work.

Hymie's mother insisted I stay at her house, so that's where I stayed. I helped her get a few things in order around the house and at the deli. I went to the studios and met with some friends, but there wasn't one position open. Many people were out of work and every position had a multitude of applications. Days and then weeks passed by quickly, no job, running short on funds and missing Muriel back home started to weigh heavy on my shoulders. I couldn't ask for a loan; I was too proud.

I was well aware that my skills were limited. I needed to rely on friends to get me a job that would provide on the job training to teach me the skills to advance. The problem was there were too many qualified people out of work and vying for positions.

I had only one ace in the hole—boxing. I decided to go and see an old friend of Hymie's, Johnny Keyes. He was once the mayor of Chinatown in New York many years ago. Cordially, Johnny greeted me. I told him that I came to the coast to see Hymie's mother.

"Danny, I never met you, but I feel like I know you. I attended many of your fights when Hymie was your manager."

"I know that you and Hymie were friends and I need to fight. Can you help me? I'm low on cash and there's no work around."

Johnny Keyes reached into his pocket and handed me some money.

"Here's one hundred dollars. I'll arrange some fights and you can pay me back after the fights."

I refused to take any money from Johnny. I didn't like borrowing money from anyone.

"I want you to come and stay with me and my wife at my home in San Bernardino. You can train there and I'll work on setting up fights."

Johnny took me to the deli to tell Mrs. Miller that I'd be staying with him for a couple weeks to train. His house as well as his wife was beautiful. The room was airy, bright, and comfortable. There was local gym nearby where I trained. I started back on my routine of beginning each day with a two mile run then headed to the gym for a work out. I was in terrible shape and not ready to fight anybody too soon. Three days later, Johnny told me that he set up a ten-round fight for Saturday night in San Francisco against Kuing Kong. It was the main event.

"Johnny, I need more time to get in better shape. How can I fight with so little training?"

"You need money, don't you? This is the best I can do to help you. If I postpone we'll lose the opportunity."

Saturday was only three days away. We packed the car and headed north up the Pacific Coast Highway. The scenery was beautiful and it distracted me temporarily from the reality of the looming fight. I knew I was in terrible shape and not ready.

There was a trainer at the arena. He took care of me in the dressing room. I entered the ring and looked across at Kong. He was muscular and toned. He took me down in the sixth round. In the dressing room, I completely broke down, trembling and crying. I was humiliated with this outcome. It wasn't me, it was awful. I wasn't ready, mentally or physically, to fight. I knew it. I was disgusted with myself for allowing Johnny to convince me to fight. I had to control myself.

The next day Johnny gave me two hundred dollars. I could care less anymore. I was where I was many times before, underneath the thumb of a crooked manager getting screwed. I started to believe that this is the way it is, boxers are f—— over by managers. I cooled off and went back to see Mrs. Miller to tell her that I was returning to New York. It was an emotional good-bye.

"I'm going to the cemetery to pay my respects to Hymie before I head back to New York."

Mrs. Miller cried and held on to me for dear life. I hated to leave her but I knew that I must. I untangled myself from her embrace, kissed her on the cheek and thanked her for her help. I stopped by Hymie's gravesite and prayed for my dear friend. I took a taxi to the Greyhound Bus Terminal and bought a one-way ticket back to New York. While riding home I vowed that I'd never fight in Los Angeles again.

The bus ride home was tedious and long, it was full and uncomfortable. People were squeezed into the narrow seats. I used the hours to reminisce about my adventures on the freight trains. When I arrived home, Muriel welcomed me warmly. She truly missed me and I missed her. We sat and talked about the recent job interviews I had and she listened intently as I replayed my painful story, the loss in San Francisco against Kuing Kong. She was deeply hurt for me. She felt my pain, we were one.

"You were out of shape and rushed by Johnny Keyes to fight. Don't let the fight haunt you. You'll have better luck next time."

My father-in-law was delighted to see me. He set me up with a job at the fish market so I could make a little cash until Irving Cohen could get some fights lined up. After work, I went to the gym and worked out with a vengeance. I'd never go into the ring again unprepared. I was determined to get into the best shape I could. If there was any chance of winning again in the ring, I had to work hard like my life depended on it.

The fights started coming, but I wasn't winning. I lost five bouts in a row. I felt washed up and my dream for the tile was out of my grasp. Irving still worked diligently to get matches for me. The little money I made for losing helped out. Each dollar I won I gave to Muriel who had a knack for making it go a long way.

Irving came to the gym and told me that I was fighting Joe Marciente a week from Saturday at Fort Hamilton Arena. Joe Marciente was a young and up and coming fighter. My workout for the next week intensified. I wanted this win to prove to others and myself that I was still a contender. The fight lasted three rounds and I walked away with a win and three hundred dollars. Two weeks later I fought Johnny Hernandez at the Broadway Arena. It was a draw after an eight-round battle. After work, Whitey was waiting for me at the gym. He handed me the sports section of the news.

> Harry Jeffra Lost Title to Sixto Escobar in Puerto Rico

It upset me to read about Jeffra's loss, but I wanted a fight against him. I figured when I beat him I'd get a shot at the title against Escobar. I increased and intensified my workout schedule. My goal was in reach for the first time.

35

It was the winter of 1939. The heating costs were astronomical and it was impossible for people to heat their homes during the frigid days and nights. The side streets were piled high with snow and the sidewalks and roads were treacherous, covered with ice. Working long hours at the fish market and long nights of intensive training at the gym was wearing me down. Sixto Escobar was out of reach for the near future. I was in the ring sparring when Irving arrived and watched me in the ring. When I finished, he was smiling, so I was hoping for good news.

"In two weeks, Baltimore Arena, fighting Harry Jeffra."

It wasn't a title fight but it was one step closer. I was surprised that Jeffra gave me a chance knowing our history. Jeffra was a gentleman and a fine boxer. This would be a good fight for both of us. Whitey started to train my mind as well as my body. Continually, he built up my confidence and my endurance. He wanted to set my mind at ease and erase any doubts I might have about the fight.

"Danny, you've fought Jeffra before and knocked him out. He'll always remember the punch that ended the round. You're in top shape and on top of your game."

On the ride to Baltimore, Muriel sat next to me in the back seat and Whitey and Irving sat in the front. I concentrated on remembering the knockout of Jeffra and the adrenaline rush I felt when I entered the ring and when I won. I longed to feel that rush again. I wanted the win. I tasted it, it was my time.

Whitey finished taping my hands, put the gloves on, and gave me a quick rubdown on my shoulders and neck. Irving wished me luck and left for his seat ringside. Quietly, Muriel sat next to me and asked Whitey if she could have a few moments alone with me. He nodded his head and stepped out. Muriel slid over close to me and put her arms around my neck.

"I want you to do what you do best, box him and win. I love you. You'll always be my champion."

Muriel made me strong. She believed in me as a boxer. I was ready to fight and win this bout. Whitey tapped on the door and came back in.

"It's time, Danny."

Muriel left for her seat and Whitey escorted me to the ring. The house was packed and the crowd was ready for a fight. Dramatically, the ring announcer made his introductions, and the crowd loved it. They went wild. The referee motioned us center ring for instructions. Jeffra and I touched gloves and went back to our corners and waited for the bell.

Jeffra jumped off his stool as the echo of the first round bell dissolved and the screams of the crowd took over. Jeffra stayed in his corner. He didn't advance to the center of the ring where I waited for him. He had a new strategy, luring me to his corner. Cautiously, I inched my way over. I didn't throw a jab or a punch, and Jeffra just stayed there bobbing and weaving like he was shadow boxing.

There were few punches thrown in that first round. As I sat on my stool, Whitey wiped me down, although I never broke a sweat and never got hit with a punch.

"Danny, what the hell is Jeffra doing? Does he think he's at the prom? He acts like he wants to dance. Take over and put him out of his misery. The crowd paid to see a fight, not a waltz."

Whitey was hilarious, but sadly true. Jeffra wasn't the same guy I fought. Still I had to be on guard, complacency was dangerous in the fight game. I was not taking any chances. Maybe he was setting me up for a knockout punch. The second round imitated the first. The referee was frustrated and yelled for us to start punching. By the third round, the crowd was standing, booing us out of the arena. I always gave the crowds a well-fought fight. I was embarrassed. The crowd felt ripped off. They wanted their money's worth. I couldn't get close enough to Jeffra to land a punch. He just kept dancing around the ring. Truly it was a dance contest. In the middle of the fifth round the referee had enough, he was tired of yelling at us to throw punches. He put his hands between us, pointed to the scoring table, and stopped the fight.

"No contest! No contest!"

The crowd went ballistic. Bottles and cups were thrown into the ring. The ring was a garbage dump by the time I left. Whitey didn't ask any questions, he just grabbed me and quickly walked me back to the dressing room. Whitey went nuts.

"What the hell was going on with Jeffra tonight?"

"What the hell is no contest?"

"It means that both of you failed to box. The referee warned several times to start boxing and no one listened."

Irving and Muriel entered the dressing room and Irving looked forlorn.

"The boxing commission has refused to give us our purse money. They feel you and Jeffra were in cahoots and deliberately didn't fight. I've schedule a meeting with them in the morning, so that you can testify. You need to tell the truth and clear your name. You came here to fight."

At ten the next morning, Whitey, Irving, and I were seated at a long table in front of the boxing commission. Harry Jeffra sat with his team on the other side of table. Neither one of us had a mark on us. The commissioner was sour and upset about the results of the match and that he had to be here on his day off. He started in on me first.

"Danny, why didn't you box and actively try to win the match?"

I was a little pissed that he accused me of no action when I tried to engage Jeffra to fight. Jeffra was defensive the entire fight, right up to the stoppage by the referee.

"Sir, I tried to be aggressive with Jeffra, but he kept his distance, running away from me and I couldn't land a punch."

The commissioner asked Jeffra questions and he was equally defensive about his actions. After two hours of grueling questioning, the commissioner and deputy excused themselves from the table. They went into a chamber to make a decision. Within fifteen minutes they returned.

"Mr. Jeffra, and Mr. London, in one week at the Baltimore Arena you will have a six-round rematch and finish the fight."

A week later, instant replay, back in the dressing room, gloves on and making my way to the ring. The local fans arrived early to watch the bout. The local papers reported me as the underdog and Jeffra on paper was the favorite.

The first round bell rung and Jeffra was a completely different fighter. His strategy turned 180 degrees. He was aggressive and threw nonstop punches. I gave them right back to him, punch for punch. It was a thrilling six-round fight. At the end, the crowd was on their feet applauding. The upsetting outcome was Jeffra won by decision. I walked to his corner and shook his hand.

Irving entered the dressing room, said that I was robbed and handed me three hundred dollars. I was robbed twice in one night. I knew I should have received a lot more.

Irving got me more fights over the next couple of years and it was the same old payday. He always had an excuse why the money wasn't enough. He was a broken record, round and round with no ending.

36

In 1941, the Second World War started. My left hand was hurting for a few years, but I continued to fight injured with that nagging sore knuckle that became a handicap and my bouts became sad results. Irving got me a fight with George Pace, the one-time champion. He was a well-known boxer with an impressive record. We were scheduled to fight in my old hometown in Coney Island.

I trained for this comeback bout with all the inspiration that my career experience allowed. I really felt strong and positive. The fact that I was fighting in my hometown and on my turf really gave me a moral boost.

I sat in the arena dressing room while Whitey taped my hands, thinking back on all the fights I had there. But tonight wasn't just another fight, it was do or die for my career.

Whitey put my gloves on and draped my robe over my shoulders. He opened the door and that familiar sound of the mumbles of a large crowd filled my ears. The walk to ring seemed like it took forever and when the fans got a glimpse of me they began to chant.

"Danny London! Danny London!"

Whitey lifted the ropes and I jumped in the ring and slowly looked in to the arena seats. The faces were of my many friends, fans, and family. They were always loyal and supportive of me throughout my whole career, win or lose.

As I scanned the seats my eyes focused on an old familiar face. The glaring lights were in my eyes but that small straw hat and pencil thin moustache was definitely the face of the one and only Doc Reiner. Was he back living the US? Did he come here to see me fight? Was it really Doc Reiner?

Muriel's bright eyes were shining when we made eye contact and she blew me a kiss and lipped, "Good luck, Danny."

The referee called us to the center of the ring and gave us our instructions. George Pace looked strong and focused and ready for the fight. He knew me all too well and this was also a big bout for him. We returned to our corners and waited for the first round bell to ring. The crowd rumbles muffled the bell as I met George Pace in the center of the ring.

I hit Pace with a solid left jab that rocked his head back and the crowd jumped to their feet, but the bad news was the pain from my aggravated knuckle shot up my left arm and lingered there for the entire first round. I was hurting and my jabs became ineffective throughout the ten-round bout.

Still with the handicap that was now apparent to Pace, Whitey and even the crowd kept George Pace leery and cautious about my boxing skills. I fought hard and felt I won the fight. The tenth-round bell sounded and we went to our corners. The ring announcer called us to the center of the ring and announced the scorer's results. George Pace won by a point in a close decision. I gave George Pace a handshake and he said, "Good fight, Danny."

The crowd was silent and then a voice from the back of the arena began to chant.

"Danny London! Danny London! Danny London!"

All the way back to the dressing room I heard the chants and I felt great, even though I lost the fight something inside me was saying, "Danny London, you're a winner."

I lost by a close decision and Irving handed me one hundred twenty-five dollars. This was the last straw—my last fight. I hung up my gloves for good.

I gave Muriel the money and told her that I quit boxing and hung up my gloves forever. She was thrilled. She watched as I tried to fulfill a dream and struggled with the business end of boxing for years.

"All the fights you fought and all the strenuous training you did for yourself and family. You gave your all to get a title fight and never got a break. You're a boxer and you won the title for a champion husband and father. I wish the breaks came your way. We need to begin a new life and forget the past."

The tears streamed down her cheeks.

EPILOGUE

The war came into full swing and young men enlisted in droves to defend our country. A good friend, Joe Henderson, hired Danny as a milkman, a union wage job. He worked for Sheffield Farms for ten years and then made a company change to Dairy Test Farms in Maspeth, Long Island, for fifteen years. The bosses he worked for treated him extremely well and after twenty-five years, he retired. Muriel and Danny moved to Pacific Grove in Monterey, California. They raised a beautiful family, two sons, Gary, their younger son, who drowned in 1972, and Michael, their older son, who lives with his wife, Wendy, in Saratoga Springs, New York. They own Mrs. London's Bake Shop. Danny has three handsome grandsons, Jason, Josh, and Max, and a beautiful granddaughter, Sophie. After Danny retired, he spent as much time as he could with the love of his life, Muriel. Danny also developed a passion for drawing and painting. He enjoyed his life and was blessed many times, with sight and sound, true love, beautiful children and grandchildren and being supported to pursue a dream. Danny was proud of his boxing career. He boxed for thirteen years, with a record of 168 fights, 120 wins, 32 lost by decision, 15 draws, and had three TKOs, but his back was never on the ring canvas. His face never had a mark on it from the fights. His childhood dream of having a cauliflower ear never came true.

He was elated about that. With all the ups and downs in his boxing career, Danny always thought of himself as a boxer; proud to be in the ring and accomplish what he did. He was thankful for the people who taught him the art of boxing and past on his knowledge. In his later years he taught and trained kids to learn the skills of boxing in Monterey, California, and Saratoga Springs, New York. Danny lived a life many just dream of with no regrets.

Danny London lived to be eighty years old. He died in 1994.

Danny London

AMATEUR RECORD OF DANNY LONDON
1928-1929

#	Opponent	Result	Round	Location
1	Al Howard	Lost	3rd	Central-"Y"
2	George Rolling	Lost	3rd	Rochester County
3	Jack Weinstein	Won	3rd	Special-Bout
4	Eddie Jacobs	Lost	3rd	Far-Rockway
5	Manny Williams	Won	3rd	Non Parel Club
6	Sam Goldberg	"No Contest"		
7	Dan Pascola	Won	4rd	Special Bout
8	Lou Pampolone	Won	4rd	Knight of St. Antony
9	Angelo Ginex	Won	3rd	Knight of St. Antony
10	Joe Fournier	Lost	3rd	New-Haven
11	Paul Klein	Lost	3rd	Rochester-County
12	Al Howard	Lost	4rd	Knight of St. Antony
13	Al Burton	Won	3rd	Knight of St. Antony
14	Joe Reno	Won	3rd	New Jersey

John J. Morabito

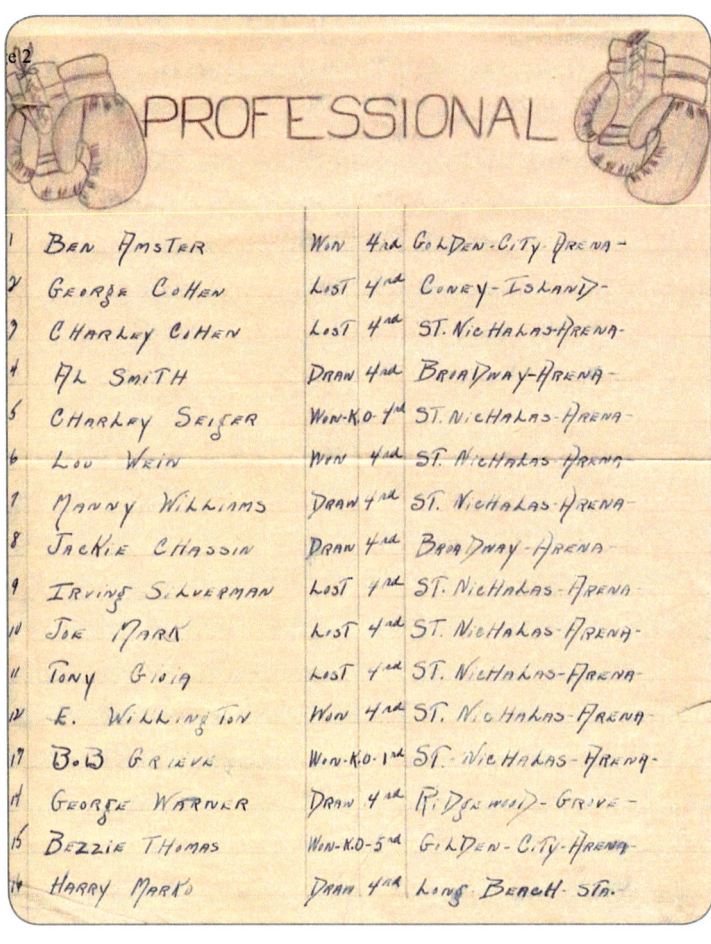

Danny London

#	Opponent	Result	Rd	Venue
17	Petey Hayes	Lost	4th	Yankee S.A.
18	Jack Kress	Win	4th	Long Beach Sta.
19	Petey Hayes	Lost	4th	Ridgewood Grove
20	Dick De-La-Cruz	Win KO 1st		Long Beach Sta.
21	Petey Hayes	Lost	4th	Broadway Arena
22	Bob Walley	Draw	4th	Broadway Arena
23	Ray Ortega	Draw	4th	Broadway Arena
24	Lou Ramo	Won KO 2nd		Rockland Palace
25	Al Smith	Lost	4th	Rockland Palace
26	Earnest Torres	Won	4th	St. Nicholas Arena
27	Lou Farber	Lost	4th	Madison Square Garden
28	Johnny Konick	Won	4th	Ridgewood Grove
29	Ira Brown	Won	4th	St. Nicholas Arena
30	Frank Rinaldi	Lost Won	4th	St. Nicholas Arena
31	Johnny Blaine	Lost	4th	Broadway Arena
32	Bob Armstrong	Won	4th	St. Nicholas Arena
33	Tony "Sugar" A.Broci	Won	4th	Yonkers Columbus S.C.
34	Tony Al Bano	Lost	4th	Ridgewood Grove
35	Sol Triose	Win	4th	Rockland Palace
36	Vincent Benta	Lost	6th	Strauchs Arena

John J. Morabito

#	Opponent	Result	Rounds	Venue
	T. Fernandez	Draw	4th	Broadway Arena
	Joe Simmonet	Win	4th	Lenox S.C.
	Joe Boggi	Lost	4th	Madison Square Garden
	Al Wolf	Win	4th	Golden City Arena
	Jim Lorenzo	Win	4th	Golden City Arena
	Sam Sanchez	Won	4th	Golden City Arena
	Al Weinstein	Win K.O. 1st		Golden City Arena
	Dave Brown	Draw	4th	Golden City Arena
	Oscar Goldman	Lost	5th	Golden City Arena
	Tony Albano	Draw	4th	Jamaica Arena
	Tom Reed	Win K.O. 3rd		Jamaica Arena
	Willie Harvey	Won K.O. 1st		New Jersey
	Barney O'Connel	Lost	5th	Jamaica Arena
50	Charley Roberts	Draw	6th	New Jersey
51	Marty Rogan	Won	6th	Staten Island
52	Mauro De La Reyes	Won K.O. 3rd		Jamaica Arena
53	Vic "Piccy" Amato	Win	6th	Staten Island
54	Mike Belluise	Lost	4th	Lenox A.C.
55	Johnny De Foe	Draw	4th	St. Nicholas Arena
56	Mike Belluise	Lost	5th	Starlight Park

Danny London

#	Opponent	Result	Rd	Venue	Date
57	Tommy Barbed	Win	4th	Coney-Island-Sta.-	
58	Joe Tass	Won-K.O.-1st		Coney-Island-Sta.-	9/15/32
59	Tony De Meno	Won	6th	Fort-Hamilton-Arena-	9/29/32
60	Jerry Mazza	List	6th	Stauch's-Arena-	10/14/32
61	Joe Pasquale	Won	4th	Jamaica-Arena-	2/6/33
62	Jack Schraldi	Won	6th	Jamaica-Arena-	2/13/33
63	Mickey Alberts	Won-K.O.-1st		Jamaica-Arena-	2/27/33
64	Phil Bruno	Won	4th	Ridgewood-Grove-	3/11/33
65	Jimmy Fantini	List	5th	Lenox Sport-Cl.B	3/14/33
66	Joe Barra	Drew	4th	Ridgewood-Grove-	4/1/33
67	Joe Doherty	List	4th	Menora-Temple-Bilding	4/5/33
68	Patsy-La-Rocco	Drawn	6th	Ridgewood-Grove-	4/13/33
69	Joe Doherty	Drawn	6th	Coney-Island-	6/12/33
70	Gene De Mont.	Won	6th	Fort-Hamilton-	9/2/33
71	Al Gillette	Drawn	6th	Coney-Island-	9/4/33
72	Max Mellen	Win-K.O.-4th		Salt-Lake-City-	9/1/33
73	Jack Twain	Win	4th	Salt-Lake-City-	10/13/33
74	Jimmy Welsh	Win-T.K.O.-3rd		Salt-Lake-City-	11/23/33
75	Leroy Gibson	Win	6th	Salt-Lake-City-	10/31/33
76	Billy West	Won-K.O.-5th		Reni-Nevada-	11/8/33

John J. Morabito

#	Opponent	Result	Rounds	Venue
37	T. Fernandez	Draw	4th	Broadway-Arena
38	Joe Simmonet	Won	4th	Lenox-S.C.
39	Joe Boggi	Lost	4th	Madison-Square-Garden
40	Al Wolf	Won	4th	Golden-City-Arena
41	Jim Lorenzo	Won	4th	Golden-City-Arena
42	Sam Sanchez	Won	4th	Golden-City-Arena
43	Al Weinstein	Win-K.O.-1st		Golden-City-Arena
44	Dave Brown	Draw	4th	Golden-City-Arena
45	Oscar Goldman	Lost	5th	Golden-City-Arena
46	Tony Albano	Draw	4th	Jamaica Arena
47	Tom Reed	Win-K.O.-3rd		Jamaica-Arena
48	Willie Harvey	Won-K.O.-4th		New Jersey
49	Barney O'Connell	Lost	5th	Jamaica-Arena
50	Charley Roberts	Draw	6th	New Jersey
51	Marty Rogan	Won	6th	Staten-Island
52	Mauro-De-La-Reyes	Won-K.O.-3rd		Jamaica-Arena
53	Vic "Piccy" Amato	Won	6th	Staten Island
54	Mike Belluise	Lost	4th	Lenox-A.C.
55	Johnny-De-Foe	Draw	4th	St. Nicholas-Arena
56	Mike Belluise	Lost	2nd	Starlight-Park

Danny London

Eddie Holmes	Won	4th	Ridgewood Grove	3/17/34
Tommy Rawson	Won	6th	Ridgewood Grove	3/24/34
Johnny Bonito	Lost	6th	Ridgewood Grove	4/7/34
Leo Dazzo	Lost	6th	Ebbets Field	7/14/34
Johnny De Foe	Lost	6th	Coney Island	
Midget St. Hilaire	Draw	8th	Rhode Island	
Tommy Howell	Won	6th	Utica, N.Y.	1/15/34
Len Monte	Lost	6th	Ridgewood Grove	12/24/34
Vic Caggiano	Won	6th	St. Nicholas Palace	1/1/35
Al Coiths	Won TKO 4th		Ridgewood Grove	2/1/35
~~John Katz~~	X		Luna Park	
Midget St. Hilaire	Won	8th	Holyoke, Mass.	2/1/35
Frankie "Kid" Corelli	Lost	6th	St. Nicholas Arena	3/1/35
Johnny Bang	Won	10th	Holyoke, Mass.	3/1/35
Lou Camps	Won	6th	St. Nicholas Arena	3/1/35
Jerry Mazza	Lost	8th	Coney Island	3/19/35
Dick Welsh	Lost	6th	St. Nicholas Arena	4/1/35
Dick Welsh	Won	6th	St. Nicholas Arena	4/9/35
John Mirabella	Won TKO 2nd		Luna Park	7/12/35
Tommy Marenge	Won	6th	Luna Park	8/14/35

John J. Morabito

#	Opponent	Result	Venue	Date
7	Diminick Nico	Won-K.O. 2nd	Luna Park	1/22/35
8	Al Todisco	Won 8th	Braddick-Bowl-N.J.	8/28/35
9	Al Ragone	Won 6th	Luna Park	9/6/35
10	Pat Robertson	Won 6th	Lenox-Club	10/16/35
11	Harry Jeffra	Won-K.O.-5th	Carlins Park-Balt-MD	4/20/35
12	Joe Rivears	Lost-K.O.By-7th	Carlins Park-Balt.M.D.	11/35
13	Herbie Hansford	Won 4th	Hollywood-Calif.-	
14	Ray Campo	Won 4th (Drawn crossed out)	Hollywood-Calif.-	
15	Deal Barnes	Won-K.O.-2nd	Hollywood-Calif.	
16	Mark Diaz	Won 6th	Hollywood-Calif.-	
17	Pete-De-Grasse	Won 6th	Hollywood-Calif.-	
18	Georgie Hansford	Won 6th	Hollywood-Calif.-	
19	Norment Quarles	Lost 10th	Oriole-Park-Balt-MD.	5/1/36
11	George Soo Basie	Won-K.O. 5th	Coney Island Vel.	June 19x
11	Sol "Tin Can" Romanelli	Won-K.O.-5th	Ciney-Island-Vel.-	Aug 1936
1	Baby Casanova	Lost-K.O.-By-3rd	Dexter-Park-	Sept 1936
10	Al Cuillo	Won 8th (Trost crossed out)	Broadway-Arena-	10/20/36
14	Al Cuillo	Lost 8th	Broadway-Arena-	1/10/36
15	Johnny Pena	Won-T.K.O.-5th	Broadway-Arena-	3/2/37
16	Varias Milking	Won-T.K.O.-4th	Hollywood-Calif	4/2/37